COMMUNICATING LOVE

Staying Close in a 24/7 Media-Saturated Society

Stephanie Bennett, Ph.D.

Linus
Publications, Inc.

Published by Linus Publications, Inc.

Deer Park, NY 11729

Front Cover Photograph, Chris Jeffries, UK

ISBN 1-60797-120-8

Printed in the United States of America.

Print Number 5   4   3   2   1

This is dedicated to the One I love.

Soli Deo gloria
Stephanie Bennett
June 2010

IV

Table of Contents

Acknowledgements vi

Foreword vii

Preface ix

Chapter 1
Where is the Love? 1

Chapter 2
Listening for Love 13

Chapter 3
The Art of Conversation 23

Chapter 4
Intimacy and Identity 37

Chapter 5
Reconcilable Differences 49

Chapter 6
Relationships on the Run 65

Chapter 7
Close Encounters 73

Chapter 8
The Wellspring 97

Appendix
IORD 123

Acknowledgements

There may be as many people I am indebted to as there are pages in this book. Acknowledging them all is impossible. I appreciate everyone who read through the manuscript and especially the friends and colleagues along the way who cheered me on. Your input was invaluable. Special thanks goes to Jon Zens, Paul Soukup, and Terry Craig whose comments and critique provided valuable help throughout the writing process.

Inspiration for this book comes from life, and my life has been blessed with the love of my dear family and friends, without whom there would be no way to understand the length and breadth and depth of love, let alone write about it. Thank you Bethany, Matthew, and Sondra for the countless opportunities you have given me to grow in love. Your faces light up my life. Ryan and Madee – my heart leaps whenever I think of you. Thank you Mom, Dad, Ruthie, Neen, Pete, John, Chris, Grandmom and Aunt Judy for the wonderful memories and ongoing love we share. Thank you, Musketeers. You know how much you mean to me. CJ, your photographs rock! Jules, Theresa, — what would I do without you two? Most of all there is Earl, my noble man – the one who has helped establish the rhythm of my days. Through thick and thin you have been there and you believed in me from the first day we met. Thank you for lettin' me be myself.

Foreword

Communication is one of those things that everybody must be involved in, but many people do not do well. Short-circuits in communication can result in everything from divorce to all-out war. Healthy communication with people can be such a great blessing, but deterioration of communication with others can be one of the heaviest burdens to carry in life.

An example of the relational frustration that can emerge from strained communications is found in Marjorie Kellogg's story, *Tell Me That You Love Me Junie Moon*. Junie tries to diffuse a tense atmosphere by making a kind remark. Arthur responds in an ugly manner, and Junie bursts out:

> The trouble, Arthur, with you is that you seldom listen to me, and when you do you don't hear, and when you do hear you hear wrong, and even when you hear right you change it so fast that it's never the same.

I'm sure all of us have had such feelings in our efforts at communicating with others. Stephanie Bennett's *Communicating Love* provides perspectives and insights that will be singularly helpful to those who wish to improve relationships by bettering their communication skills.

The realm of communication does not lend itself to simplistic formulas and easy-to-follow steps. And no wonder, for each setting where communication occurs involves the many intangibles connected to the personalities and circumstances. Stephanie knows this and does a beautiful job of speaking generally enough to allow for plenty of flexibility, yet specifically enough that her readers can relate what is said to their peculiar setting.

One of the most profound books I have ever read is Thomas Dubay's *Caring: A Biblical Theology of Community*. In it he makes these far-reaching observations:

> If it does not matter to me what my sisters or brothers think about significant issues, I can be sure I do not love them as I ought . . . . Even more, we value the opinions of those we

love. If I do not really care what my brother thinks, I had better doubt that I love my brother.

This is the burden of *Communicating Love*. A great deal of time is spent in our lives pursuing or avoiding communication. If we truly love other people then we must grow in our ability to listen to others, to explore the thoughts of others, and to value the concerns of others. This book will go a long way in stimulating and facilitating such important growth in our personal lives.

— Jon Zens, Editor, *Searching Together* and author of *A Church Building Every ½ Mile: What Makes American Christianity Tick?* and *What's With Paul & Women? Unlocking the Cultural Background to 1 Timothy 2*

Preface

Let's get it out of the way up front.

This is not a book about technology; it is not a book about how to use text messages or email to multi-task your relationships. This is a book about the mystery, complexity *and blessedness* of that beautiful thing we call *love*. The pages that follow were written with the intention of helping readers keep relationships strong and love alive in the midst of a crazy, upside-down, world. It is an invitation to explore the simple ways and daily choices we each can make to put an end to the madness that stems from our busy, multi-tasking lifestyles. Exploration of this subject may best be seen as an expedition – a road we will travel together – writer and reader, enjoying the time, learning, growing, pondering, and finding our way through the vast territory of human relationship. Along the way I trust that we each will end with some wisdom gained; you with the inspiration and motivation to continue to invest in your relationships, I, with the same, gleaned from finally putting my thoughts about this subject down on paper. It is my ardent hope to provide some help in making sense of the practical ways to keep love flourishing in all of our relationships, whether they are marriages, friendships, or in the family.

One of the most ironic things about love is that in spite of the fact of its primary importance in our lives, many of the choices we make in communicating love are the most expedient ones, and we give little – or no – thought to the ramifications of these choices. As long as our message is received, we feel as though we've communicated properly. And actually, come to think of it — whether we knock on a friend's door, pick up the cell phone to call our spouse, send a text message to a distant family member, or email to a neighbor, a word *is a word* is a word, right? *Is it?*

Not exactly. What we say is enormously affected by how we say it, and this includes the mode of communication we choose. For instance, the convenience and efficiency of technological devices and broadband connections are extremely helpful in everyday life, but they change *everything*. Texting, social networking, GPS devices – each of these has become almost indispensable to our ability to communicate with those we love. Think about it: Can you imagine going on a long drive by yourself and not having your mobile phone close by? These days, most people can't. How about typing up a report, memo, or term paper with a little bottle of white-out next to you there on the desk? (I wonder if half of the people reading this paragraph will not even know what white-out is!) Many activities and tasks that are made possible by advanced communication technologies are so helpful that it is hardly possible to think about living without them. And, when these technologies are used to help us communicate, you can bet the way we manage our relationships is influenced. Consider some particulars:

A cell phone makes long distance relationships sing with the sound of immediacy, and the melody is so much more intense than the sparse connection a mere email might bring. Yet, is this connection point an adequate substitution for an embrace or face-to-face conversation in the park? Or, the joy a daily email and photo exchange via the Internet brings to help keep a long-distance relationship alive, nurturing the love and commitment that a husband and wife who have been separated by business or military obligations. How could these technologies be anything but helpful to our relationships? More on that question in a moment. Whether relational or work-related, the arguments for extending the reach of the human communication through technology's devices are compelling. Why use a typewriter and white-out when a word processing program makes the process one hundred times easier and much less time consuming? The time saved might make it possible to go on vacation more often or even work from home — which can only be a good thing. *Right?*

Technology is great. . . *In some ways.* The ability to extend human reach by means of a pen, or the voice by means of a cell phone, or the strength of our legs by means of a train or automobile each have benefits to which human beings have long since become accustomed. It is the *other* ways – the ways in which a technological solution seems to take matters out of our hands and foist an answer we wouldn't choose – that technology isn't so great. And, when it comes to influencing our relationships, it is imperative that we look closely at the ways the technological solution does not serve us best.

Using the new media to stay connected sounds like a good idea, but there are definite and distinctive parts of the process of communication that are missed when human beings begin to rely on devices to mediate our relationships instead of choosing more reliable, but often inconvenient, method of face-to-face communication. The demise of dialogue and true conversation is just one aspect of this conundrum. There are others. For instance, the limitations of having to pick one from among only ten font choices on a pull down menu might not feel terribly restrictive. We are able to turn a blind eye to the inconvenience of not being able to choose exactly what we want because of the vast convenience of using a computer. We are apt to set aside the frustration of not being able to type outside a template box for a company newsletter because, after all, the template makes the entire project just so much easier than cutting and pasting a hard copy. However, when our love language is limited by similar menu choices or by the screen space on a blackberry, we may not be as satisfied but will opt to use it anyway for the sake of expedience. Or, when there are 700 emails in our box, many with jangling needs and not enough time to address any of them with proper focus, we may begin to notice the importance of using our technologies wisely instead of letting them use us. Without understanding how the devices we use shape our communication process, we run the risk of losing many of the essential components that make our relationships so rich. When we use technology's devices without considering what is most appropriate, simple frustration may lead to complete communication breakdown. It is here that the real problems with our media-saturated society are hidden, and it is here that they begin to emerge.

Communicating Love addresses the need to reassess the prominent place that we have given technology in our everyday life, and sets out to help readers with the most basic of life's essentials – primary relationships. We will take a close, careful look at the way love is communicated in the midst of our busy, multi-tasking lives and attempt to uncover ways in which love might be *better* communicated. In fact, keeping relationships intact and thriving is the goal of all that is written in the pages that follow. Just the fact that you have picked up this book, I know that you, dear reader, want to reach this goal and – be assured — it is my desire to help. In an effort to do so I have set about to structure the book according to the fascinating and unpredictable dynamics of life that are part of the human experience, and have chosen the ending passage of T.S. Elliot's classic poem, "Choruses from The Rock," to introduce the ideas of each chapter. Why Elliot? His poetry is exquisite, *just like love*. It often takes a while to understand Elliot's poems, but with a bit of patience and care the words begin to leap from the pages and we are drawn into the drama and delight of the poet's eyes, seeing life in such a way that one might miss without it. Sometimes, we do things just for the sake of beauty. Why take two extra minutes to stare at the strawberry sky as the sun goes down on a beautiful beach in the tropics? It's more than relaxing; it is lovely. The words of T.S. Elliot are part of the loveliness of life. They ring true and have long provided me with a framework for thinking about what it means to be human, what it means to be a lover, what it means to be loved. His words speak of the need for wisdom, and along with love, wisdom is perhaps the most necessary element in keeping our relationships, strong, vibrant, and growing. So, I invite you to join the conversation, to journey with me through the ensuing pages to take a thoughtful, serious look at a topic that is not only important to us all, but perhaps the very core and capstone of civilization, — something so fundamental and natural it is easily overlooked – the simplicity, beauty, and flourishing of healthy relationships.

From: Choruses from "The Rock."

The endless cycle of idea and action,
Endless invention, endless experiment,
Brings knowledge of motion, but not of stillness;
Knowledge of speech, but not of silence;
Knowledge of words, and ignorance of the Word.
All our knowledge brings us nearer to our ignorance,
All our ignorance brings us nearer to death,
But nearness to death no nearer to God.
Where is the Life we have lost in living?
Where is the wisdom we have lost in knowledge?
Where is the knowledge we have lost in information?
The cycles of Heaven in twenty centuries
Bring us farther from God and nearer to the Dust.[1]

---

1. Eliot, T. S. Choruses from "*The Rock.*" *Collected Poems,*1909-1935.New York: Harcourt, Brace, c. 1936.179.

Chapter 1

Where is the Love?

The endless cycle of idea and action,
Endless invention, endless experiment,

Is there such a thing as "true love"? Many of society's sages would never deny it, but even a cursory look at the state of contemporary relationships creates a disconnect between our collective social knowledge and what we experience. Divorce, broken friendships, bitter family feuds, church splits – all these have historic precedence, but today seem exacerbated by an inability to get past offense, hyper-individualism, and the utter breakdown of communication.

As a topic of informal dialogue, love has never left the table, but neither has it been in the forefront of public discussion. Rather than speak of *true love* our poets and pundits continually call attention to the over-sexed hookups of Hollywood's glitterati or the fuzzy, feel-good experience of love "at-first-sight." But as a subject of serious discussion, love often takes a back seat to the glut of information-soaked gibberish purported by gossip columnists and entertainment writers who enjoy lavishing the latest break-ups and make-ups upon their viewers. It's true – instead of being approached seriously, the subject of *love* often sits quietly in the shadows while other more savory subjects are pranced out onto the runway with the spotlight constantly shining and the public begging for more. So with you, I ask: Is there such a thing as *true love,* and if so, why is it demeaned this way? Why isn't love taken seriously?

In the last sixty years our collective understanding of love has increasingly come from depictions of love through mass media. Images and representations of love that we see on the silver screen, the television, and the Internet seem to take precedence over the lives of actual people that we know and see living firm and secure marriages. As a direct correlate, much of our inability to effectively communicate love stems from the way the mass media have fictionalized love and redefined it in terms that are far beneath its beauty and reality. For this reason we will begin our journey by taking a look at the different types of love and the various ways love has been defined through the ages. Rather than head immediately to discerning the *language* of love, it is important to look closely at the subject of our communication, that is, love itself. Before we go further, though – let's be clear about what we are discussing here. Are we speaking about romance, friendship, or sexual union? Yes, yes ... and yes. Love comes in many shapes and forms, so let's take a cursory look at some of the various types of love and get more in-depth later. There are four most basic types of love, each may best be described by the ancient Greek word that describes them:

+ **Eros** – Romantic love

+ **Storge** – Affection

+ **Philia** – Brotherly love

+ **Agape** – Divine love or Charity[2]

Romantic love is one way of describing *eros.* The word has the same etymology as *erotic,* and, while it certainly includes the sexual aspect, it is better typified in the state of "being in love." It is a love that is occupied with the well being of the beloved. *Storge,* the affectionate type of love may best be described by the love of a parent for a child. *Philia* finds its root in the relationships among

---

2 C.S. Lewis describes Charity as "gift love" in his classic book on the subject called *The Four Loves.*

friends. Each of these types of love has clearly distinguishable features, but all of them have one thing in common: they are conditional. *Eros* loves *because*.... Because you are beautiful, because you are kind, because I am attracted to you; Eros says, I love you, *because.* Both *Storge* and *Philio* love *if.* If you and I are compatible; if you agree with me; if you give me a lift to the airport; if you do what I say; if *you love me. Agape* is sometimes known as charity, but in its contemporary definition charity falls far short of the breadth and depth of agape. *Agape* loves *in spite of* . . . In spite of the fact that you have disobeyed, in spite of your rebellion, in spite of your inability to be consistent, your indifference. *Agape* loves with unconditional acceptance; *Agape* is the love of God.

There are actually many other expressions of love, and many other words for love mentioned throughout literature and in various cultures. A few other Greek words used to describe love include the following: *Mania* – possessive, dependant love; *Ludus* – game-playing love. Some expressions of love, such as *bestowal love* are similar to, or overlap with, romantic love. This type of love is that which sees the value and glory of another person.[3] *Courtly love* has to do with chivalric or service-oriented love. We think of this kind of love when we remember the troubadours of the late 11th century who traveled the county side singing in honor and service of the courtly ladies of their knights.

We won't be able to go over all the aspects of every kind of love in the world, but it is important to take some time to discuss the elements of what has universally been deemed *true love.* We've seen and experienced the counterfeits and illusions, and hopefully experienced the "real thing," but the idea of true love has long been a bit of an anomaly. Can true love be true even if it doesn't last? Is true love an indicator of lasting relationship? No matter how many love stories we hear or how many **movies** we watch with love as **its** theme, we tend never to grow tired of hearing more. Like a favorite pair of slippers, we return again and again to the familiar idea of true love, but are often left chilly and confused with each new breakup or heartache. Perhaps it might be more beneficial to

---

3 Singer, Irving. (1984). *Plato to Luther*, vol. 1 of *The Nature of Love*, 2nd ed. Chicago: University of Chicago Press.

look at true love in light of the qualities we've come to expect of it. Let's take a closer look at those aspects of love that *we can count on as real, lasting, and worthy* – and explore the ways we can make sure to keep them at the forefront of all our important relationships.

The Aspects of Love

Despite the fact that love can never be reduced to a list, *it is* possible to discover the elements of true love and take time daily to apply them to all our relationships. To begin, let's look at the unifying factors in all these types of love. It doesn't matter if it is friendship or the love between a parent and child or romantic love or that which occurs between siblings — there are several aspects of love that form a common thread. Perhaps the most obvious one is the ability to value another person for who they are and to seek the best for them. The value we place upon the other, **as other**, and our desire to love them and be loved is a beautiful thing, but unless that love is effectively communicated to the other, the relationship will not grow and will remain less than its potential. In fact, even in a relationship that is firmly established, quite often the love does not prove strong enough – or real enough – to keep the relationship thriving. Part of the reason for this sad fact is that love is not a thing; it is not a noun. Love is alive, and anything that is living needs tending to for it to remain vibrant. The quandary, however, is this: Just how do we communicate our love to others? We make mistakes, muddle our words, do and say stupid, unloving things sometimes, don't we? For love to be strong and a relationship to stay intact, is it really necessary to communicate perfectly? Absolutely not, but the key is – *to communicate*; and the type of communication necessary involves some very basic building blocks.

Unfortunately, the most important of these skills is often overlooked or taken for granted. There are three, in particular, that are rarely mentioned but carry great weight in determining whether or not our relationship will be the lasting kind. The first is *listening*. Listening may seem so obvious that it does not need mentioning, but if your friend or spouse loves to talk and *you prefer peace and quiet*, listening can be a most difficult thing to do. Or, if you tend to be particularly busy and your friend has much time on his hands, listening may not be terribly easy. There is an art to listening, and ways to improve listening skills. This, we shall explore in a minute. Now, let's look at another important aspect of love – passion.

Passion may seem like another "no-brainer." It would seem that above all other aspects of love, passion is lauded and pranced before our eyes with graphic precision. Everyday when steamy, passionate expressions of love fill our television screens, blanket our billboards, and submerge us in instant replays of passionate carnal knowledge. Passion is most certainly a major part of love, but it is also grossly misunderstood. Whether it is sexually charged passion or a fervent devotion to one's child or parent, passion packs a big punch, but how many of us recognize that passion has two sides? Let's look at the root of the word, and we'll see why. The etymology of the word passion is found in the Greek *pathos*. It involves deep feeling, zeal, suffering, and *pain*! Yes, long-standing love relationships involve suffering for *and with* the other. (More about passion later when we discuss the *eros* in more detail.)

Along with listening and passion there are everyday features of love that involve simple consideration of the other. This umbrella term covers a myriad of small, relatively insignificant acts of kindness and care. It may sound less important than the other aspects, but consideration of the other in all things is part of the way love is communicated every single day. Caring deeply about the concerns and needs of another as well as the many mundane elements of everyday life such as house cleaning, shopping, food preparation – all of these are a part of bringing full expression to love's table, for it is when we are performing these mundane acts that love becomes visible. This makes much sense because love is a verb. It is actionable. However, these simple acts of caring for another can present a big problem when they are not reciprocated or when the needs of the other totally eclipse our own.

Whether in friendship, marriage, or among siblings, communicating love necessitates our listening to the other, allowing passion to have its proper place, and consideration of the other; that is, taking the other into account in the midst of our plans, needs, and desires. Notice, each of these aspects involves "the other." True love is much more oriented toward 'the other' than our popular culture and instincts may lead us to believe. And when it comes to suffering — let's face it — there is often discomfort and inconvenience when one must put the needs of another before one's own needs. A baby that is up all night long with a fever cannot give anything back to a parent, but that parent will give up sleep and get by on less than enough energy the next day for love's sake.

A friend who is moving from one house to another and needs help loading and unloading the truck may not present a great problem or inconvenience, but what about when it wreaks havoc in our schedule? To be sure, love is wedded to our emotions, but if it is to last, it will be not be dependent upon the ebb and flow of our daily moods and circumstances. *Feelings* are not the ground of love.

True love is motivated by something much greater than our senses. It involves accepting and embracing the whole person, giving that friend, lover, or child the freedom to form their own thoughts, ideas, and words. This type of love emanates from a place much deeper and more vast than what a finite being could manage. It flows from the center of God's own heart, for love is God's idea. He is the Author of Love. God created us for Himself and to be in relationship with others. He is the initiator of love. God could have created the world in any number of ways, but decided to make it a place where people are drawn into relationship, where woman and man need each other to survive. Although there may be times when a broken heart may tempt us to plummet into a bubble of isolation, we were not meant to be alone. *Eros, storge* and *philia* are beautiful, but ultimately cannot stand on their own strength for very long. The gifts of natural love need to be transformed by His perfect love, *apage.* When human love is transformed by *Agape,* it is almost as if it is converted, and it is there, in the midst of the Divine touch, that love is no longer left to the whim and fancy of human caprice or the undulating tides of mere emotion. It is there, that our frail, often-faltering and conditional love has the potential to become something larger than itself; something beautiful, rich, and truly out-of-this-world!

Love's Illusion in Pop Culture

Part of the reason for the disconnect between the idea of love and one's ability to experience it lies in the fact that being in a loving relationship is far different from *falling in love.* Or, with friends, the feelings of warmth and congeniality are often quite different from the outworking of friendship in everyday life. What occurs each day may best be explained as the nitty-gritty of love — the place where love lives. But the effusive, grandiose "idea" of love exists right along side it, and though the idea is a very nice one, *it often gets in the way of the reality.*

The **idea** of love has to do with the feelings of exalted worth and hope – even intoxication – with another person; the **experience** of it in everyday life has to do with the daily outworking and actuality of *being* with another. Working side-by-side, living in close proximity, sharing space – whether in marriage, friendship, parenthood, or the church – the feelings associated with love are often far different from the fact of walking in everyday relationship. While it's true that the idea of true love has long been romanticized, in the last 25 years the very idea of it has lost much of its luster. With rises in divorce rates and ever-increasing one-night get-togethers becoming the norm, it would seem that speaking of love as something that is "true" has become something of pop culture myth in this generation. Inexhaustible pages of text provide countless tips for finding love, but exalting the essence of love is not a popular subject. The truest elements of love are rarely discussed. Realities of love such as sacrifice, service, unrealized dreams, even suffering and other mortifications of the self are not *sexy,* but are all a part of lasting, loving relationships. Household chores, cleaning, cooking, and tending to the other's most basic needs when they are sick or unable to do so for themselves — all of these everyday activities are part of the house of love. From the simple to the sublime, *love* is about "the other," but even the most loving person must find a way to communicate this love in ways that the other can understand.

So where are these false ideas of love generated? Often, they stem from a combination of what we've read and what we've seen in the media. In recent history, at least since the days of radio, popular culture has been functioning as the arbiter of love, mediating the idea of love to the masses through advertisements, drama, and the endless varieties of entertainment programming. After radio came television. Everything from cartoons and the commercialization of love in such characters as Betty Boop, Barbie and Ken, and *Friends* to the entrée of sexy soap stars, rock legend lifestyles, and film portrayals of romance have affected our collective idea of love. Depictions of glamorous people falling in love have filled the small screen and entered the nation's living rooms for many years. Today, the pernicious influence of the Internet delivering pornography right to one's den with the simple click of a mouse has become a new way that popular culture sets the tone for our collective notion of love. True love has been "losing money" for many years, and today it is clear that the definition of it has morphed into something that is far different from the loyal, kind, faithful, patient, and compassionate qualities that once defined it.

The music industry is another place we see the gap. So often the longing for true love is capsized and flung into an ocean of confusion and fantasy through popular music. Countless songs remind us of the ache for true love. One that comes quickly to mind is a lilting tune from the 1970's, a song sung by Roberta Flack and Donny Hathaway. The wistful voices of this soulful duet put the probing questions to melody, begging audiences to listen, but not really expecting an answer.

"Where is the Love, you said was mine, all mine, 'til the end of time?

Was it just a lie?

Where is the Love?[4]

Such disappointment and despair have never been exempt from the reality of love, but today the questions are coupled with the added angst of throw-away friendships and one night hook-ups as increasingly normative features in the makeup of society. Unfortunately, the enthusiasm for singing about love's lonely track record or bemoaning the way relationships so easily fail does not match the ways we are able to articulate our need for the reality of love. Inexhaustible pages of text provide countless tips for finding love, hiding our love affairs, and making physical love more satisfying, but how many of these pages discuss the elements one must bring to love's table rather than collapsing the process into a mechanism for "getting what we want"?

Love is more than an idea, more than a feeling, and more about giving than *getting what we want*. In her book, *Gravity and Grace,* Simone Weil discusses love in this way and considers the difference between the illusion and the reality of love. She writes: "Real love consents to the independent freedom of other people, whereas our imagination often leads us to live in a fantasy

---

4 *WHERE IS THE LOVE?* – by Roberta Flack and Donny Hathaway (1971) Lyrics listed at end of the book. Have a listen: http://www.youtube.com/watch?v=6Sl-MHhEJxI

world in which we script and control a person's words and actions."[5]
Popular culture focuses on the rewards and benefits of love, rarely
on the more challenging hard work of relationship maintenance.

The very idea that love involves work may seem ludicrous.
Work is just not sexy. But, if it's loving, long-lasting relationships
that we seek, we will have to reckon with love, and the genuine
version of love takes a bit more than wishing or hoping that
"everything will work out" in the end. Love takes perseverance
and patience. This brings us back to the garden metaphor. Just as
the patience is necessary as farmers "wait for the rain," it is necessary
to wait patiently for significant relationships to deepen and bear
fruit. The process of cultivating a relationship is similar to the
tilling, fertilizing, daily watering, and weeding of the garden we
envisioned earlier. It is impossible to enjoy the ripe and delicious
fruit and vegetables of our garden without taking the time to nurture
what we've planted. Red, ripe, juicy tomatoes don't just fall out of
the air. They are connected to the vine and the dirt and the spade.
They grow slowly and contain the vitamins, color, and tantalizing
taste of the hard work of waiting for the harvest. If love is to be
more than an ideal or unrealizable dream then it must stay
connected to the earth. In other words, love must be firmly rooted
in the reality of everyday life – that is, everyday, not intermittent.
Yet, it must also find its root in a place that is untouched by the
havoc of the unpredictable universe of human emotions and the
ups and downs of everyday life. The good news is that there is
such a place; it is the river of God's love. The river of God is one
that does not dry up when feelings fade or adversity comes. But
where is that river, and how does one stay current in its lively
stream? Ah, that is one of the underlying themes of this book, one
we will touch upon time and again, but before we go deeper, let's
continue to explore some of the reasons for the gap between the
idea of love and its reality. Below are five of the most prominent
reasons why our dream relationships die before they ever have a
chance to fly. I'm calling them the Five Fallacies.

1. We live in the illusion of perfection.

2. We leap past important steps of relationship development.

---

5 Simone Weil, *Gravity and Grace*, NY: Routledge 1987. p. 9.

3. We live for tomorrow or yesterday and lose out on the present moment.

4. We look for love in all the wrong places.

5. We mistake the other for "the one" who will make us whole.

Each of these problems will be covered throughout the remainder of this book, but I'd like to point out one final fallacy that wrecks havoc in so many relationships. It's the idea that love is true "as long as it lasts." Such a temporary, frail version of love hardly seems worthy of all the attention we give it. There are several distinct reasons for this, the first having more to do with the disintegration and breakdown of the self-as-a-part-of-community, and that is a deeply significant aspect of the problem but not the subject of this particular book. Another exceedingly important reason for the proliferation of these fallacies lies in something quite a bit simpler, and that is in an inability to communicate love effectively. To that subject we will now turn.

Communicating Love

True love, both as an idea and an experience may be out of fashion, but it is not far outside our grasp. Worthwhile relationships that are long-lasting and rich are much within our reach. Learning how to most effectively communicate love in all of our primary relationships is both an investment and a life-long learning process, one that may have more to do with our ability to enjoy love for a lifetime. More than anything else it requires the motivation and desire to do so. Grappling with the tensions and inconsistencies is nothing new; it has been going on for as long as history is recorded. The ongoing "Great Conversation" about life, love, and meaning has been taking place among the thinkers for at least 2,500 years. From Plato's *Phaedrus* and the *Nicomachean Ethics* of Aristotle to Augustine's *Confessions*, the wealth of Shakespearean plays, Austen's novels, and beyond, the idea of true love and its counterfeits has been contemplated and rehearsed with much zeal. In fact, discussion of love may be found in annals going even farther back to the great corpus of Chinese and Greek mythology or the Hebrew Scriptures. The Preacher's *Song of Solomon* gives due attention to the regaling of true love, its clarity and devotion — even its propensity toward possessiveness and jealousy. We are not alone in our quandaries. The challenges of the 21st may be different, but the longing for love is the same. The answers may not be easy, but the questions are worthy ones. In fact, learning to ask the right questions about relationships affords each of us a greater chance at finding meaningful answers, but without understanding what these questions are, or locating the goals of our communication process, the prospect of arriving at our desired destination grows dim.

To establish and maintain flourishing relationships we must first grapple with love's mysteries and be willing to embark on a journey that includes both self-discovery and the joy of getting to really know the other. So, let's make a pact here to examine the ways our experience of love differs from our ideas of love and seek to cultivate strong, vibrant relationships that will last. Let us continue to wrestle with the difficult questions and dive right into the deep waters that will help us take love from an endless cycle of idea and abstraction to a living and fruitful reality in everyday life.

Part of the ability to communicate love effectively is understanding that ultimately the source of love is not our own hearts or minds. Love flows from a source other than our own finite selves. It is like a gravitational pull and whether a person is tapped into the fathomless, eternal supply of divine love or not, the "laws of love," like gravity, are always in operation. For some, that pull is so strong it causes them to act in ways that are destructive, even violent — much like a child "acts out" in grade school because he/she is harboring anger or hidden emotional pain. But — even for believers – without an outlet to express and walk in that love, essentially, we are all crippled. It's as if our hands are tied, our feet are bound up, and the truest longings of our hearts are thrown in a little black box that is tightly shut and locked away somewhere only to be found once our life is over and Someone recovers it, shakes off the dust and brings out the only Key that will open it up. Why should we live behind locked doors until we die? We were not meant to.

That said, let's take a look at some of the ways we can protect and encourage our love relationships to flourish. Believe it or not, they don't start with learning how to say the words, "I love you," but with a deep and residing silence — a rich ground in which the roots of relationship become established and may eventually blossom into deep and lasting love. Why silence? Turn the page... let's find out.

Chapter 2

Listening for Love

Brings knowledge of motion, but not of stillness;
Knowledge of speech, but not of silence;

Have you ever squinted while reading the newspaper? No? Well, than perhaps your vision is without flaw. However, if you are one of the millions of people with less than perfect vision it will be frustrating for you to try and read without your glasses. Why? Everything is out of focus. The words blur on the page. Happily, a simple corrective lens adjusts the vision and alleviates the frustration. What about the focus necessary to properly hear what another is saying?

The human brain has an amazing ability to filter and focus, so that even in a loud, crowded room it is possible to be engaged in an intense one-on-one conversation. But too much noise has an impact on the quality of our listening skills. Although we cannot "hear" it with our ears, visual stimuli such as computer screens, magazines, and televisions hooked up to every restaurant and waiting rooms are all types of noise that provide information and stimulation to our brains. Surely these media are often informative and enjoyable, but they also keep us distracted. As we add our own personal mobile media such as Blackberries, iPods, and cell phones, the ability to stay focused becomes even more compromised.

While some of the sounds and images require no response, combined, they become part of a vast glut of information that surrounds us. In fact, we are nearly submerged in information, so much, that it is part of our environment. The concept of our media as our environment may be difficult at first, but think of it this way: Instead of rolling hills and running streams surrounding us, we are surrounded by a steady stream of information flowing from the many media outlets in our world. This information fills our homes, our cars, and public places. The media environment may also be referred to as a *media* landscape — something that we are "in." Whether we live in rural Iowa or a busy metropolis, mediated messages are increasingly saturating our minds and they have an increasing impact on our ability to focus. So, what does all this have to do with communicating love? Think of it: How many times have you taken a call on your cell phone while in the middle of a conversation with someone else? Or, perhaps you enjoy the text messaging feature on the phone and engage in an exchange while driving. It sounds crazy, but people do it. Maybe you have never experienced trying to navigate two conversations at once, but my guess is that you have, and you know that you cannot truly focus on both.

Typically, we don't think of the need for focus when discussing our auditory function, but in a noise-drenched world of media it is time to consider the need for more intentional, focused listening. The fact is, much of communicating effectively depends on the ability to listen to what the other is saying. Listening is the largest percentage of time each day that we spend communicating.[6] Most communication scholars agree that the percentage of time that the average individual spends communicating each day using their listening skills falls between the range of 75% and 93%.[7] Listening is essential to maintaining coherence in the conversation; without it, little chance to communicate lovingly exists.

In this chapter, we will take a look at the ways that the *art* of listening can make a positive impact on how relationships develop and how love is effectively communicated. First, we will look at the elements of listening and seek to apply them to our own particular communication

---

6. Birdwhistell, Raymond. (1970). *Kenesics and Context.* Philadelphia, PA: University of Pennsylvania Press.

7. Anthropologist Ray Birdwhistell and psychologist Albert Mehraian are among the early social science theorists who discovered these results in their research.

style. Next, we will discuss the important role of silence and solitude and the ways learning to listen can help bring back the ability to focus into our lives. With focused listening, the ability to communicate love becomes much easier. To start, let's look at why listening is such an important part of the communication process.

Listening is that part of the communication process that comprises the largest percentage of the entire time we spend communicating each day.[8] It stands to reason that if one cannot hear, or is distracted by an overload of sound or information, there will be difficulty listening and in the ensuing, necessary elements of interpreting meaning and responding. All of this points to an increased need to be better listeners. There are many listening techniques that you might employ if you think you are not a good listener, but the least contrived and quickest route to improvement is simply to listen intentionally.

Listening with Intention

The idea of listening with intention immediately seems redundant for to listen we must go beyond hearing; however, it is notable that as much as people think they are good listeners, listening skills are not inherent; they *must* be learned. If our hearing is normal, we can listen to anything, right? Not so fast. Hearing is the first, and perhaps most important step, to becoming a good listener. It stands to reason that if one cannot hear, or is distracted by an overload of sound, there will be difficulty listening and in the ensuing, necessary elements of interpreting meaning and responding in loving, meaningful ways. Hearing has to do with our auditory function – the ability to connect with sound – but listening is much more intentional. It is not automatic. To listen to someone or something involves several steps. Once heard, we must attend to what is being said, and then interpret what it means, and finally, respond. It is here that active listening take place.

Impediments to listening have long hindered relationships for reasons prior to the present cluttered media landscape. As I see it, there are two major reasons that people do not listen —

---

8. It is generally believed that the amount of time people spend listening each day eclipses the other communication acts with the following breakout: 17% reading, 13% writing, 16% speaking and a whopping 53% listening.

lack of interest in what is being said and self-focus. Clearly, messages sent back and forth from one person to another are not all neatly packaged, processed, and put forth in a set or uniform method. Rather, what we consider "the message," or the substance of the communication is constantly in flux, and dependent upon numerous variables. These variables are considerable. Personality, culture, "mood," attitude, state of mind, scheduling conflicts, external stressors such as work or sickness, interior unrest or confusion, lack of clarity, and numerous other factors come into play, affecting each person's ability to make adjustments to maintain the amount of focus necessary to really listen to another. These may be even more difficult to change, but they must be addressed if we are to become better listeners.

Today, however, the ability to be a good listener is exacerbated by the multiplicity of all that glut of information that we just mentioned. The umbrella term that covers all the aural and visual stimuli is called noise. Even perfect hearing does not filter out the extraneous noise of too much information, and unfortunately, no special lens or mechanism exists that helps us focus on what the people we love most are saying. *Noise* gets in the way of our ability to communicate love effectively because it so often hampers our ability to listen.

Listening with the heart

Ears are important, but not more significant than the heart. Typically, we don't think of the "heart" when we think about what it means to listen. But listening *relationally* means leaning in to who the person is, listening to what they are saying that is beyond the actual words. Certainly, we're not talking about the blood-pumping organ located in the center of the chest, but that place in the depth of the human soul that is the center of emotion. The heart and the mind are intimately connected, and what is needed in our noise-drenched world of media is a desire to truly listen, to really hear what the other is saying. This takes focus. The fact is, much of our ability to communicate effectively depends on the ability to not only hear to what the other is saying, but to listen to the hopes, dreams, desires, and feelings that are behind the words. This takes a good deal more attention than reading a text message in the midst of a work day. It takes being attentive to the non-verbal communication cues and is very much a part of the push-and-pull of everyday relationships.

Contributing to this push-and-pull are all those aspects of our communication environment that reduce our ability to hear and attend to what someone is saying, things such as: the medium used, the context, the ability and skill of those doing the speaking, the nature of the exchange, the desire and enthusiasm of the participants, and a myriad of physical and psychological variables. In fact, without the tension involved in each opposing pole it is hardly possible that there could be a fullness of speech at all. This is the beauty of dialogue and a good part of the reason it must not be left off as new modes of communication arise. The 20th century philosopher and social theorist, Jacques Ellul, concurred in his estimation of the value of the spoken word and the inherent essentiality of speech. Here, he wrote, "Speech does not take its pattern directly from what there is 'to say,' it creates in addition a sphere of unexpectedness, a wonderful flowering which adorns, enriches, and ennobles what I have to say, instead of expressing it directly, flatly, and exactly."[9] How lovely it is to be on the receiving end of the kind of speech that really communicates our love to another. Equally, it is enriching and life-giving to be able to communicate in this way toward others.

The Sound of Silence

Silence can "cut like a knife" when someone has been wronged in a relationship and communication is shut down. Unfortunately, it is often used as a weapon relationally to shut out someone that we love. Let's not do that. However, used properly, as a reprieve or respectful way to consider more carefully the thoughts (or accusations!) of the other, silence can be a most useful tool in communicating love. First, silence helps us to become better listeners. It can work miracles in a relationship if it is doled out in small measures and used a means by which we stop talking to really consider what the other is saying. This is because listening involves much more than hearing the words of others; it involves

---

9. Ellul, Jacques. (1985). *The Humiliation of the Word.* (Trans. Hanks, J. M.) Grand Rapids, MI: Eerdmans. P. 17.

being able to "hear" what is unspoken. People we love tell us as much or more with the great nonverbal aspect of communication than the words they speak, but in order "to hear" them, we have got to include regular intervals of silence and solitude into our lives and be willing to refrain from filling every possible moment with words. David Runcorn suggests that solitude is a necessary means of detachment from the world and explains its connection with our ability to truly love one another. He writes:

> Detachment enables us to stand back. It enables us to gain a wider perspective. It is not the withdrawal of love and involvement, but a more careful and discerning offering of it. Without detachment a sensitive love for this world, in all its complexity and pain, will be overwhelmed and drained empty.[10]

Certainly, love does not want to be too detached, but learning to "give space" is precisely where silence may be used as a healing salve to bind up the wounds of too much talk that has been said in haste. While I am most assuredly not advocating complete silence, or a silence that "shuts down" and ignores the other, the healing properties found in solitude are often the simplest and most easily accessible solution to repairing the walls that divide two people. Eugene Peterson intimates as much in the following:

> The world, for all its vaunted celebration of sensuality, is a relentless anesthetic, obliterating feelings by ugliness and noise, draining the beauty out of people and things so that they are functionally efficient, scornful of the aesthetic except as it can be contained in a museum or a flower garden. Our senses require healing and rehabilitation so that they are adequate for receiving and responding to visitations and appearances of the [Holy] Spirit.[11]

In many ways silence is disappearing from our world, not in the vast open spaces of American plains or the deep woods, but in the cities and in the suburbs. This is sad, because solitude is necessary in order to come to peace with one's self. It is essential, in fact, when trying to make sense of our feelings and concerns, and has deep, residing effect on how we relate to others.

---

10. Runcorn, David. *A Circle of Quiet,* InterVarstiy Press, IL 1990.

11. Eugene Peterson, *Subversive Spirituality,* Eerdmans, Grand Rapids, 1997. pp 13-14.

Without a proper amount of solitude in our lives there is little time to reflect, or even consider, what the other might be thinking or feeling. It is in solitude that we are able to peel away the layered masks we wear and come to a place of self revelation where we "see" ourselves in true light, for we cannot know who we are without spending time reflecting, contemplating — thinking about who we are. It is there, springing from regular solitude and silence that we are better prepared to bring an authentic self to the table of relationship. These interior activities are natural and essential to the flourishing of the human soul, but they are thwarted daily, not only by the psychological means of self-protection we exhibit by closing ourselves off from others, but by the need to make a living and exist in the world, Indeed, today, these very human needs are exacerbated by the flood of information that we each have to deal with. Thomas Merton says as much when he relates this concept to his fellow monks:

> It is in solitude that I find the gentleness with which I am truly to love my brothers . . . Solitude and silence teach me to love my brothers for what they are, not for what they say.[12]

Learning to communicate love to those we love involves loving who they actually are instead of our false idea or wishful thinking. Merton's emphasis on the need for solitude to sort out our motives is especially important in light of the swelling technological wave of the mid-twentieth century in which he wrote, but may be even more salient to the current media environment. We need to speak *to the person* we love, not to *the idea* of the person. We need to listen *to the person* we love with ears attuned to who they are, for without acknowledging and appreciating the person, our relationship is quickly reduced to a fantasy and has little chance of survival. Awareness of the personhood of the lover or friend affects the way we communicate our love, but it necessitates looking beyond the masks and external distractions that keep us at emotional and spiritual distance from one another. To start, it means getting in touch with one's own interior, an endeavor much supported by the regular practice of solitude. Thomas Merton's insight on these matters are well worth quoting.

---

12. Merton, Thomas. *Seeds of Contemplation.* p. 41

When society is made up of men who know no interior solitude it can no longer be held together by love: and consequently it is held together by a violent and abusive authority. But when men are violently deprived of the solitude and freedom which are their due, the society in which they live becomes putrid; it festers with servility, resentment, and hate. No amount of technological progress will cure the hatred that eats away the vitality of materialistic society like a spiritual cancer. The only cure is, and must always be, spiritual (pp x-xi).[13]

Thankfully, there is a spiritual cure which we will address more specifically in chapter 8, but as we lean in to listen carefully to the other we begin to

No one means to be overwhelmed or stressed by too much media, but that does not negate the reality of its relentless press against our souls. Incoming information demands that we listen, attend to, and assign meaning to it, but when we are unable to do so, a sense of overwhelming "maxing out" easily ensues. Seven hundred emails waiting in the ebox, twenty text messages, several phone calls to return, and an attempt to find time to go for a walk or a run with a friend is not unheard of; in fact, it is rapidly becoming the norm. So, what is to be done with all of this extraneous information?

Some of it may be processed rather easily by the extraordinary capacity of our brains to filter out unimportant details, but these days the magnitude of this information is unprecedented and it requires much more time to process than in the past. While individual choices concerning use of these devices may vary somewhat, recent statistics point to the fact that once we begin using our iPhones, Blackberries and other personal mobile media we easily become dependent upon them, and, no matter how accustomed one is to the cacophony, no matter how well we manage it, the new media environment dramatically changes our social patterns, greatly impacting the way we conduct our relationships. How so? There are numerous ways. Have you ever been the recipient of an invitation to meet for coffee or have dinner and the other person is interrupted from incoming calls or text messages? This might be the one of the most apparent examples of rude behavior, but it often happens unintentionally. In fact, perhaps we've not only been on the receiving end of this type of behavior, but sometimes find ourselves caught in the same trap. We forget to turn our cell phone off and an important call comes in. There's their image on our little screen. Should we ignore it? Maybe, but what if it is an emergency? These are the thoughts that muddle with our minds and tamper with our social protocols of politeness.

---

13. Merton, Thomas. (1979). "Love and Need: Is Love a Package or a Message?" [in] Anderson, R., Cissna, K., & Arnett, R. eds. (1994). *The reach of dialogue: confirmation, voice, and community*. Creskhill, New Jersey: Hampton Press (pp 249-254)

notice who they really are, and instead of communicating from our limited perspective alone, we begin to see them from a wider vantage point. For this, some silence and solitude are necessary, for from the bed of silence leaps speech. Conversation, rich and flowing, is made more possible when we have spent time in solitude considering the other as other, instead of simply what they do or what they bring to us. We'll delve much more deeply into this connection in a few moments, but for now, let's take a look at the importance of growing in the art of conversation.

Chapter 3

The Art of Conversation

Knowledge of words, and ignorance of the Word.
All our knowledge brings us nearer to our ignorance,

You have gone to the movies, taken bike rides together and spent hours texting and emailing, but you still don't feel as though you know him well enough to make a long-term commitment. Yet, the more time you spend together, the more you long to get to know this man. Why can't you get into a deep discussion? Sometimes you may even feel as though you have to pry his emotions out of him. Or, perhaps it is the other way around. Maybe *she* is the one who is reticent to open up and share spontaneously, from the heart. Perhaps it is a friend who enjoys spending time at the movies, hiking, or shopping with you, but your conversations never seem to go much deeper than the activity at hand. If you wonder when you will ever move from chit-chat, ballgames, movies, and externalities to openly sharing what's on your minds and hearts, let's press on!

First of all, you are not alone. Many people grow to love others but find it difficult to carry on regular conversation. It is often easier to talk about the movies, the weather, gossip – anything but what's on your heart – and fill the time instead with television, computing, and shared activities. To talk about the relationship may be even more difficult. Part of the problem is that so many of us have been socialized into *not talking*. Many Baby Boomers and GenXers learned to sit passively in front of the television screen. The Millennials (a.k.a. Generation Next) seem to opt for the smaller screen, but either way, the art of conversation is not easily practiced while staring at a screen, no matter how large or small it is.

Having a conversation with someone is the most natural thing in the world — people do it all the time. In fact, it is so natural it may cause one to wonder how it warrants an entire section in a book about communication. Simply: conversation can be tough. You and I both know it. Sometimes it just doesn't work, and carrying on a conversation seems a bit like pulling teeth. This is due to many factors, the risk of rejection not the least, but mostly so because conversation requires a person to venture outside of ourselves and get beyond the cares and concerns that take up much of our mind space each day. It requires us to engage the other – to get beyond the everyday necessities of schedules, bills, cooking, cleaning, and work. It involves self-disclosure. Conversation builds the commitment we make to each other as friends, lovers, or family, and knits us with each other in something that cannot be achieved by ourselves: *relationship*. The fact is, relationship is largely established through conversation.

It is important to note that all conversation is not in-depth, deeply relational, or intimate. Much of interpersonal communication is not especially "relationship talk," but routine communication, that is, the "stuff" of everyday life. This is what is normally referred to as "small talk" and is essential to the building of intimacy and quality in relationships, but also important to the ongoing fabric and tenor of a relationship. Julia Wood and Steve Duck (2006) suggested that small talk serves multiple, simultaneous functions, emphasizing that "whatever the character of a particular relationship, you can be sure that it was established primarily by routine, ordinary communication that, over time, shaped it into what it is" (p. 8). This is the "stuff" of which relationship is made! It is the very fiber of the relationship. Julia Wood claims that conversation *is* the relationship, and explains as well, that "communication embodies relationships."[14] In the process

---

14. Wood, J. and Duck, S. (2006) *Composing Relationships*. CA: Thompson-Wadsworth. P. 33.

of communication, whether verbal or nonverbal, as conversation flows we "represent, or symbolize, what a relationship is, what it stands for, what is important in it."[15] While there are other means of embodying relationship, conversation is a primary one.

Among the many benefits of cultivating strong conversational skills is that the act of conversation frees us from the self-absorption that is part of the common experience of being human. Instead of concentrating on what's happening in my life, conversation allows us to listen to our friend and focus on what is happening in *her* life. The very act of conversation forces each participant to think beyond their own concerns. One may even say that conversation delivers us from the temptation of being completely me-centered. Certainly, conversation won't automatically accomplish this, but it is one step on the path to self-discovery and relational health. Kathleen Norris describes it as curing the problem of self-focus because it frees us from "the presumption of coming to this table [of fellowship] for solace only, and not for strength, for pardon only, and not for renewal."[16] Thus, conversation can help set the tone for mutuality in relationship. Without mutuality a relationship is one-sided. This is no fun at all and not the makings of long-term love.

Conversational Flow

As everyone knows who has tried to carry on a conversation and failed miserably, there is an art to it. Conversation must flow for it to be an enjoyable part of relationship, and when it does there is almost nothing better. In many ways, "flow" is inexplicable. There is an element of mystery to a good conversation. Chemistry, timing, and the unprogrammed exchange of ideas, feelings, dreams, and desires help to create this flow, but there is one main element in establishing this flow, and that is mutuality. Yes, mutuality, again.

What is this term "mutuality?" What does it mean? Mutuality has to do with support and empathy, but may best be understood by considering its opposite. Think about how easy it is to feel completely on the giving side of a relationship, receiving very little of the other in return. Or, consider what it feels like if you are only on the

---

15. Ibid.
16. Norris, Acedia, p. 142.

receiving end of a relationship and never allowed to give anything. Both can be extremely frustrating places to stand, for to be in a relationship that grows there must be giving *and* receiving — a mutual "give and take." Some have been taught that "it is more blessed to give then receive," and have wrongly perceived that being on the receiving end of a relationship is selfish or flat-out wrong. This is simply not the case. It takes humility to be able to receive a gift and grace to say, "thank you." When that gift is not wrapped in a package with ribbons and bows but is the trust one gives you in sharing himself or herself, this gift is even more valuable. "Receiving" the other as a gift means acceptance of what your friend or lover is sharing about himself; it does not necessarily mean "agreement." Receiving him or her paves the way for intimacy, the subject we'll discuss in greater detail in the next chapter.

Finally, this "give and take" in conversation reminds us that we are not alone, and that being in this world means being *with* others. We need others to help us know ourselves better, and the give and take of conversation works well toward that end. The way Kathleen Norris talks about this in her book, *Acedia,* is most helpful when she writes that conversation "promises to help me distinguish between fruitful self-knowledge and sterile self-consciousness."[17] Isn't *that* the truth?

Ultimately, if we want to maintain strong and fruitful relationships it is important to reckon with the fact that the time spent together in conversation with another is the stuff of which most relationships are made. It is not time wasted, nor is it superfluous. Think of the phrase that you just read: "in conversation." In a conversation you are somewhere. *You are together.* The place is not as significant as is the situation. Whether on a crowded bus heading toward the city or a quiet beach walking beneath the stars, together two can converse and find a place *with* each other.

Dialogue

Another way to talk about conversation is to speak of *dialogue.* Simply put, to dialogue means, to "talk." When we dialogue with one another we converse, exchange ideas, and let the conversation

---

17. Norris, Kathleen. (2008) *Acedia and Me.* USA: Riverhead Books.

flow, but dialogue is a particular type of conversation. The etymology of the word will help us understand why it is special. The first part of the word is *Dia;* it comes from the Greek, meaning "through." The other part of dia, *Logue,* has a Latin etymology, which means having to do with "tongue" or language. In dialogue, we get through to the other by way of language. In other words, what is opaque and mystifying about the other becomes clear when we dialogue. Dialogue may be conceived as something two or more people do together to move from the isolation of the self to interaction and shared experience with the other. Of it, French philosopher Jacques Ellul writes, " . . . a dialogue implies reserve, tension, contradiction, argument back and forth."[18] Does it seem odd to read that contradiction and tension are a part of healthy conversational practice? It may, indeed. Nevertheless, all of these elements are part of the dialectical tensions that may make life a bit more complicated, but definitely more interesting.

While conversation is essential to our ability to communicate love, dialogue often has less to do with the actual words we use, the mistakes we make, or the number of times we can steer away from disagreement. Rather, it has much more to do with what kind of person we bring to the relationship. It has to do with our willingness to step outside of our own comfort zone and look for ways to get through our own "stuff" to meet with another in the joy and wonder of conversation. Placing an emphasis on dialogue as integral to the process of communicating love helps to bring fruitfulness to the relationship and builds a greater sense of commonality between two people. It involves both words and nonverbal communication behavior. Corey Anton describes the words we use to meet one another in conversation as "living words," explaining that:

> Words surround and engulf us, and they can be set in a kind of relief only momentarily. Never mere figures against a background, living words are themselves a continuous backgrounding. They do not happen within situations as much as make situations possible; situations can be what they are only because of words. That's why the expression, 'we were in a conversation' makes good sense.[19]

---

18. *Ellul,* 1994, pp. 121-122. and *Prayer,* 1970; p. 133.

19. Corey Anton, *Wide-Eyed* June 2008. Vol. 1 No. 3. CA: Santa Monica. P. 21

Living words may be shared in a letter or an email, but they are most alive when dealing with a living being. Engaging in face-to-face dialogue is perhaps the most enriching way to have a conversation. It helps erase the boundaries that our finite and fearful selves so often create and experience as alienating. The sound of a loved one's voice can be music to our ears because it draws us into the power of their personal presence. Their words are colored with the nuance of their particular voice and touch us in ways that their thoughts may hold captive. Our words bring us together. Walter Ong writes: "What words do is precisely annihilate the in-betweenness which separates you from me and me from you. When I speak to you I am inviting you to enter into my consciousness, and I am entering into yours."[20] Thus, the opportunity for communion exists as dialogue is advanced. Communion – although there are numerous levels of this "coming into union" with another —- involves oneness, and it is an aspect of close relationship that comes about primarily through face-to-face communication and the shared experience of language.

Dialogue helps us know the other, as other, and we do this in many ways, one of which is making space for the other to speak. This involves listening deeply to both the words and what is not spoken. We learn much about each other by paying attention to the pauses, silences, and lack of response. Philosophers have long noted the necessity of silence as an integral part of speech. Some, such as Max Picard (1952), frame the dialectical tension of the spoken word and silence as a metaphor of life and death, correlating the notion of silence to darkness or to death, itself.[21] Picard's writing is poetic and his philosophy resonates with the importance of the human voice. Here, the mid-20th century philosopher whose work is in the existential vein of Gabriel Marcel, places a high premium on the interconnectedness of silence and speech as a building block of personal identity and relationship development. According to Picard, "speech must remain in relationship with the silence from which it raised itself up. It belongs to human nature that speech should turn back to silence, for it belongs to human nature to return to the place whence it has come"(p. 21).

---

20. Ong, Walter. *The Mystery and Power of the Word.* P. 5.

21. Picard's Hegelian and Heiddeggarian leanings are evident in his ontological approach to silence and speech, particularly in regard to Hegel's conception of being as spirit.

Contending that "silence is present in language . . . even after language has arisen out of silence" (p. 22), Picard associates personal security and strength of human relationship with an awareness of silence, suggesting that

> the world of language is built over and above the world of silence. Language can only enjoy security as it moves about freely in words and ideas in so far as the broad world of silence is stretched out below. From the breadth of silence language learns to achieve its own breadth; silence is for language what the net stretched out taut below him is forth tightrope walker. (p. 22)

Picard's poetic words exemplify the kind of creativity he is concerned about losing in a world without silence. His polemic against noise is evident throughout his writings, but is not due to a romantic desire to go "back to nature." What he termed the "substance" of silence is a prerequisite for the substance that must emerge from words that are uttered. He explained that

> there is no silent substance in the world today. All things are present all the time in an atmosphere of noisy rebelliousness, and man, who has lost the silence in which to sink the all-too-many, all-too-present multitude of things, allows them to evaporate and vanish in the all consuming emptiness of language.[22]

Other communication researchers such as Edward Hall (1959) see in the entire elaborated system of culture that meanings are typically found in context, a context that has developed over time. Understanding the context of a conversation is part of the dialogic process, as well. Hall saw all of culture as communication – even the "culture" of everyday life and gives as an example, the typical "everyday talk" between a husband and wife. There is a silent or unspoken message a husband sends when coming home from the office changes when greeting his wife with a bit of a raised pitch or a grumble. The husband's greeting could be spoken in a variety of ways in the nonverbal sense, each with a different meaning; the most important point may be that even in the case of the seemingly simplest of messages, communication is very complex and the limitations of various devices and the ways they are used may inhibit

---

22. Picard, Max. (1952). *The world of silence.* Chicago: Henry Regevery Company. p. 56.

discretion, judgment, and understanding in interpersonal communication. The words the husband speaks may be clearly the same as every other day, but his stance, tone, and expression "speak" more clearly than the words.

Another example of the importance of context in developing rich dialogic exchange exists in the findings of Yale and MIT graduate, Eric Brende, whose auto-ethnographic study living amidst a community of Amish farmers in Pennsylvania's Lancaster County garnered much insight about the communication that takes place in the context of culture itself. Living and working with the Amish for a period of 12 months, Brende (2004) noted the ways in which relationships were built without words among this subculture that avoids new technology almost completely. As he observed his own reactions to the low-tech way in which the Amish threshing crew worked, Brende observed the way in which the "lulls" in the midst of each day's work fostered a sense of belonging, meaningful conversation, and authentic community. He wrote:

> The work was heavy and the day long, yes. But there was something pleasantly haphazard about the scheduling; there were lulls. Lulls waiting between wagonloads. Lulls caused by lack of coordination of the persons overseeing, if anyone was overseeing. Lulls for eating and drinking. Lulls here, lulls there. [. . .] these gaps could easily have been overlooked. The lulls did not constitute mere empty time; conversation, for instance, often continued unabated when the work stopped. Lulls were part of the natural flow of human activity and rhythm. They were a testimony to genuine human leisure. (p. 158)

When applied to the advancement of dialogue in our primary relationships, the observations of Brende, Hall, and Wood point to the need for close, careful observation of the other, and deep listening.

Silence is Golden

Without a bed of silence from which speech may emerge, the possibility of dialogue between two people becomes more and more remote. Without it, in fact, all speech may be relegated to the instrumental and utilitarian ends. That is, instead of taking the time to lean in to the other and really hear what they are saying, our conversations may be regularly reduced to interactions that coordinate activity. What time is dinner – six o'clock. What are we having – pot roast and salad. What time are you coming home – I'll be there by six. Instead, it is important to take a look at how the spoken language (i.e, speech and silence together), in all its dialectical beauty and power, is one of the building blocks of meaning, love, intimacy, and relationship, in general.

It is not possible to exhaust the subject of dialogue in one small section of a book about communicating love, but it is necessary to include one other aspect of the subject. This is the matter of listening deeply. Listening deeply means that we will that when engaged in dialogue attend to the facial expression, gestures, posture, and all of the other nonverbal means of communication.

Self-Disclosure

"Communication involves making space in the world for one another."[23]

Self-disclosure is simply sharing personal information, but there are different levels of self-disclosure and different patterns. The process of disclosing feelings, ideas, desires, and dreams involves a willingness to reveal oneself and is perhaps the most important aspect in cultivating close relationship. In many ways self-disclosure is a means of making space for another in one's heart. By opening up and sharing what is in our own hearts we invite others in, giving them entrée to our lives, but willingness to open up and share about oneself is easier for some people than others. Typically, we may think of those who find it easy to reveal personal information as exceptionally confident people, and those that are reticent as shy or lacking self-esteem. These stereotypical ideas of the way people share are only partially legitimate. Some find it easier to speak incessantly of themselves, giving little space for the other to share. Strong self-disclosers may do so for social validation or the desire to boast or gain sympathy. Others, more hesitant to disclose themselves may simply feel more comfortable waiting for the other to reveal personal information first. Either way, self-disclosure involves risk, and risk is necessary in order for the possibilities of relationship to grow,

---

23. Durham-Peters, Jon. (1999) *Speaking into the Air.* Chicago, IL: University of Chicago Press. p. 30.

Self disclosure does not necessarily mean revealing dark or steamy facts about oneself, but it *is* a matter of sharing *personal* information. For self-disclosure to become a part of an ongoing norm in a close relationship basic communication skills are necessary, the foundation of which is always trust. It is here where we must engage our listening skills most intentionally, for self-disclosure involves risk – the risk of being misunderstood, rejected, or even mocked. Listening (as it relates to both the interpersonal and intrapersonal) is the primary function in the process of building trust and establishing conversation coherence. Communication scholars largely agree that this is key: "During a communication event I take in and process 'messages,' from you (intrapersonal). I use these messages to create meaning (intrapersonal); and I provide you with a response that lets you know the meaning I have created (relational). You do the same. By continuously and simultaneously listening carefully, we use one another's response to monitor our progress toward understanding and to modify subsequent communicative choices, if necessary." (p. 225)[24] In many ways this is a very natural, built-in process. Generally, people don't have to think about listening, certainly not as a separate skill, but in this hyper-technologized age of myriad distractions it is something that may require more intentionality for surely it is a major part of building trust and growing in relationship.

There are many ways to think about self-disclosure. In the 1960's, psychologist Sidney Jourard wrote *The Transparent Self,* lauding the benefits of total transparency. Jourard encouraged self-disclosure as a means to gain relational health as well as health of the whole person. He advanced the need for being honest – totally honest – about our emotional state. Other researchers in the field of communication found that this type of emotionally driven disclosure was overrated, and could even be counterproductive to the development of lasting relationships.

Love does not mandate that we reveal every slight nuance of thought. In fact, concealment may be equally important. What, you say? That sounds so dishonest! How can concealing something be part of communicating love? Here, concealment does not refer to keeping important information from others, particularly honest,

---

24. Rhodes, S. C. (1993). *Listening: A relational process.* In Wolvin, A. (Ed.) (1993).

open, declarations of affection or confessions of wrong-doing. This kind of concealment has to do with the dialectical nature of relationships, that is, the need to manage opposite, but simultaneous psychological needs. An example of this is the internal tension involved in needed personal space while at the same time wanting to spend time with one's friend or spouse. Another of the tensions involved in all relationships is the ongoing need in interpersonal communication for both openness and concealment in self-disclosure.[25] Neil Postman (1976) emphasized the need to embrace this dialectical tension as an important part of a civilized society. He wrote that

> Concealment is one of the important functions of language, and on no account should it be dismissed categorically. As I have tried to make clear earlier, semantic environments have legitimate and necessary purposes of their own which do not always coincide with the particular and pressing needs of every individual within them. One of the main purposes of many of our semantic environments, for example, is to help us maintain a minimum level of civility in conducting our affairs. Civility requires not that we deny our feelings, only that we keep them to ourselves when they are not relevant to the situation at hand. Contrary to what many people believe, Freud does not teach us that we are "better off" when we express our deepest feelings. He teaches exactly the opposite: those civilizations impossible without inhibition. Silence, reticence, restraint, and yes, even dishonesty can be great virtues, in certain circumstances. They are, for example, frequently necessary in order for people to work together harmoniously. (Stewart, 2006, p. 58)

We, in the West seem so committed to being true to ourselves, when in actuality we mistake our "self" for our feelings, which can (and do!) change everyday. This is not love, nor is it healthy self-disclosure. Rather, the effusive sharing of every nuance of feeling is

---

25. Everett M. Rogers (1994) described this dialectic in terms of relational negotiation explaining that interpersonal relationships best exist as a rhythm. The ebb and flow of openness and expression gives way to assimilation. Then, the flow and change is followed by a temporary quiet. Other tensions of risk and anxiety lead to temporary balance and security. Other prominent scholars concur and have advanced research in the area of relational dialectics such as Baxter and Montgomery, 1998; Petronio, 2002; Postman, 1976; Rogers, 1995.

sheer, mere emotionalism. We cannot be led by our emotions without setting ourselves (and our relationships) up for much confusion and loss. Of American Emotionalism and love Laura Smit writes: "We live in a tell-all society, and we tend to assume that our romantic relationships must be founded on complete self-disclosure – not a self disclosure taking place slowly, over time, or at least over the length of the courtship, but an immediate self-disclosure that holds nothing back from the first date onward."[26] Whether or not we consider ourselves "big" self-disclosers or are more private about sharing information about ourselves, we must work toward opening ourselves up to greater breadth and depth of self disclosure with those we say we love. This is where openness thrives. Total openness may not always be possible, but if

The reasons we are so apt to get caught up in the rush and rants of our technological circus are numerous. One is the aforementioned fun factor. Catching up with an old high school buddy after thirty years through a social networking site can be a blast! Plus, using our personal mobile media for social interaction helps to break out of the feeling of isolation, and that is often very good. Still other reasons have much more to do with basic questions of identity and purpose. For many, being totally saturated in busyness with more people than one life can possibly accommodate is a means of social validation. Instead of Descartes' axiom, "I think, there for I am," we are easily led into associating the number of people we know with our identity in a sort of "I click, therefore I am" mentality. We used to hear the same about print media and television, but now the popular phrase has been transferred to the world of social networking. "You don't exist unless you exist on facebook." What a lie!

it is a goal, relationship partners can always be working toward it.

Ultimately, conversation, self-disclosure, and dialogue are part of an interpersonal communication process that pave the way for relationships to grow and love to flourish. Whether that love is of the friendship kind, between family members, or of the steamy passionate category of healthy romance and marriage, relationships take us on a journey which will sometimes seem rocky. To communicate love effectively we will have to learn how to travel together through terrain that is not always stable – there will be mountains, valleys, rocks, stones, rivers, and hills – perhaps even some caverns, but if we determine to see this uneven landscape as an adventure, we will find strength for the journey.

26.Smit, Laura A. (2005). *Loves Me, Loves Me Not: The Ethics of Unrequited Love.* Grand Rapids, MI: Baker Academic.

Travel Tips for Relational Conversation

As we continue on this journey of life some of the ways to begin to strengthen conversational coherence in our relationships is to first set realistic goals and expectations. It is unreasonable to expect to advance from a marriage with little conversation to one that is flowing in it overnight. There are steps to be taken, each building upon the next. First, you might start by sharing something you are feeling or making an observation that reveals a little something about yourself.

Next, it is important to be intentional about protecting the art of conversation from becoming eclipsed by a universe of means. By becoming more mindful of the ways our tools may undermine our desire for strong, resilient, and intimate relationships, it may help us to foster more competent and relational interpersonal communication behavior, not just in our own lives, but in society at large. From a very practical standpoint, this means, among other things, that we must really listen. For that, we need to remember that silence is connected to speech. It also means that we avoid the temptation to drive the beautiful mystery of human relationship into a technological cul-de-sac. What does this mean? By resisting the desire to maintain a constant connection, and instead wait, plan, and look forward to a quality face-to-face conversation, we each can take a stand for preserving the uniqueness of the individual while at the same time being true to ourselves. Instead of following the herd and allowing close relationships to dissipate through the constant mediation of our technological tools, we are better positioned to engage in, and maintain, strong, long-lasting relationships that are authentic, intimate, and protected against the many storms that come our way.

As our personal mobile media are used with greater dependency and often substituted for communication occurring in traditional settings, it becomes even more important to set aside time for discussion and dialogue that occur in less public face-to-face settings. If we can agree that the power of language does not reside merely in message transference, but in the fullness of speech, it makes much sense to expand the ways in which interpersonal communication occurs instead of allowing it to be limited by always opting for convenience or . . . the most efficient means of carrying on a conversation.

If the conversation you'd like to start is with someone you hardly know or have just met, try asking an informational question. Asking for directions is a low-risk way of starting up a conversation. If that falls flat, try using something that is in the news as a conversation starter. Current events, the weather, or even a bit of humor can help break the ice and start up a conversation. To go deeper in conversation involves greater risk, but the risk is worthwhile.

Once the conversation is rolling, why not use the direct approach of sharing a bit of information about yourself? This often helps the other feel more comfortable and usually there will be reciprocity. For instance, if you say something like "I'm from Rhode Island and it takes some time for the summer sun to warm us up. We even have chilly days in June, but here in South Florida it seems you never need a jacket, — even in February." With a comment like that you are likely to get any number of responses, but it is very likely that you'll be on the receiving end of one that reciprocates, offering such personal information as: "Oh, you're from New England? I am from Ohio originally, which can get very cold in the winter, but we've usually got great weather by May. When did you move here?" And you're off!

Another important point to remember is that when you are searching for a way to start a conversation, be sure to avoid the formulaic lines that make people cringe and rarely produce lively conversation. How do you know if you are doing this? It starts with being true to who you are. Then, always be sure to key in on the nonverbal communication cues you are receiving from the other. Wait for an opening. Most importantly remember that the individual with whom you are speaking is a person, not a thing. A conversation should not be a means to gain favor or recognition from the other; it is a pathway into knowing that one better. Words, fitly spoken, properly weighed and weighted, provide meaning and great delight in the conversation arts; they would do well not to be wasted on sheer utility. Endeavoring to know another person well is a noble goal. It lays waste to the largely Western idea that productivity, efficiency and material success are the most worthy ventures. But to know another person and love them well is something that does not garner a paycheck, gain recognition for oneself, or establish a person as worthy and valuable. What it does is lead to happiness and purpose. It helps us know ourselves better. It helps us stay sane in an insane world. Plunge in. Take chances in conversation. Don't hold back. Love is worth it.

Chapter 4

Intimacy and Identity

All our knowledge brings us nearer to our ignorance,
All our ignorance brings us nearer to death,

Deep, closely-knit relationships can satisfy the soul like nothing else. Lifelong friendships, romance that stays lively and strong, brothers and sisters who seem more like best friends – these are a major part of life's reward, but they require commitment and intimacy.

Intimate love is not a great mystery, but it does not come easily. There are many things that can thwart intimacy, from a wrong word spoken in haste to infidelity. Also, intimacy does not become a reality if we are set on maintaining perfect control of our schedule, style, and status quo. This is because of the nature of love itself. Love is more than a feeling or a state of mind. Love is transformative; it is a powerful agent that does not adjust to our own convenience and particular comfort zones. Love is a reality that changes *everything*. To *know love* — to experience its inexplicable richness we must be willing to be changed. In fact, this may be the number one reason so many people fail to experience intimacy with others, and the primary reason for the desperately unsatisfying, miserable fascination with Saturday night hookups and one-night stands.

Intimacy is something all people crave even if they have managed to shut off the desire by convincing themselves that it is unattainable or not worth the effort or potential emotional pain. This, of subject, is not an easy venture, because *you and I were made for love.* It's true! We were *created by Love* and *for Love's sake.* No matter how we try to protect ourselves from the risks of opening our lives to others, love is always there in the background, pursuing us, stirring up desire, leading the way toward transformation. This may the very reason so many people numb themselves with the party lifestyle. Without true love, we tend to throw ourselves into activities that cloak the pain and emptiness of a life without meaningful, intimate relationships. Before we get any farther, let's take a look at the golden threads that are necessary to build intimacy.

- Openness

- Passion

- Identity – healthy sense of who you are (self)

You may wish that we would begin by discussing passion, but without openness there is little hope for long-lasting passion. The good news is that rich or poor, trim or heavy, well-educated or not, all three of these elements are within the reach of every one. Regardless of gender, financial situation, or communication skills, every single human being is capable of laying hold of these three things. It is not red roses, fancy jewelry, or romantic getaways that build intimacy. It is the willingness to be open and take risks to truly love others that will pave the road to long and lasting marriages, friendships, and family harmony. You may be reticent or shy — uncomfortable with sharing too much about yourself. How, you say, can I learn to be open if it is not in my nature? Ah, now we are ready to move to the next section: How to communicate in ways that let the other know that you are ready for love.

Let's go!

Openness

To be open is necessarily the complete opposite of being closed. Open people show they are open in many ways. Body language, eye contact, an open, ready smile – all these nonverbal cues help communicate to others that you are willing to share a conversation – ready, perhaps, to share your life. There are levels of openness, all of which require various levels of making oneself vulnerable, and right now I am not speaking about complete transparency. To be totally transparent requires the greatest level of risk, and it is savored for the very closest of relationships as they deepen into lasting love. Though some friends or lovers may wish it was so, total transparency is not the same as openness; it is not necessary that every nuance of feeling or opinion is shared in order for openness to be operating in a relationship. Openness is more a state of the heart. It is a bit like leaving the door to your house unlocked when you are expecting guests for dinner, or putting out a welcome mat or wreath on the door. When your friends arrive, everything says: "Glad you're here! C'mon in." On the other hand, if you are sitting with a friend over a cup of coffee and you turn on the television or leaf through your favorite magazine while she is talking, you are sending a signal to her that is quite the opposite of openness. You may, in fact, *be open*, but you will not likely find much success in your conversation, and you will definitely not be about the business of cultivating closeness. Openness means you will listen and be favorably disposed toward your friend, not ready to judge or leap on her every word with a critical response. This type of communication behavior is known as empathic listening —that is, listening without judging or trying to correct the other. Listening empathically does not mean that there will never be a time to offer constructive criticism. Perhaps there will, and there most certainly is a need for speaking the truth, in love. However, empathic listening helps to nurture openness; it sets the tone for the other to feel safe about disclosing information and feelings, both about oneself, and about the relationship. Without empathic listening, those you love may never feel it is safe enough to be completely honest. When we are open – torso leaning in, eyes connecting with eyes, following her words with true attention and listening with empathy – we communicate openness nonverbally. Without even speaking a word we speak volumes, and by sending the right messages we are more likely to build rich, lasting friendships. This conversational style of communication incorporates nonverbal cues that let the other know you are truly *there* – not distracted or half-listening.

Perhaps the biggest hindrance to openness is fear – fear of revealing something that the other will mock or reject. Everywhere we look people are giving up intimacy because of fear. Fearful of landing at the bottom of the heap, fearful of not being chosen, fearful of being left alone or outrightly rejected – there are numerous fears. This is why intimacy must begin with the deep assurance and experience of total acceptance. How does one overcome the many fears? St. John tells us that "Perfect love casts out fear."[27] It destroys it, stomps on it, removes it from the picture and totally overcomes it. Henri Nouwen discusses this perfection, pointing to the source of Love, in God:

> When St. John says that fear is driven out by perfect love, he points to a love that comes from God, a divine love. He does not speak about human affection, psychological compatibility, mutual attraction, or deep interpersonal feelings. All of that has its value and beauty, but the perfect love about which St. John speaks embraces and transcends all feelings, emotions, and passions. The perfect love that drives out all fear is the divine love in which we are invited to participate.[28]

An invitation to participate in relationship is always at our doorstep. Sometimes, we simply do not have eyes to see it. Rather than waiting for a "special someone" to ride in on a white horse, why not initiate an invitation to participate in friendship? Start by sharing a bit more about your self than you normally might. Often, reciprocity is the result. When you share, the other is likely to share something in return, but it must start with openness. Self-disclosure is one of the ways intimate relationship grows, and although there are various patterns of self-disclosure, it is an essential element in all relationships; without it, it is difficult for love to flourish into true, satisfying intimacy. As love begins to blossom and the layers of self-disclosure begin to unfold, it is passion's turn to rise. Strong desire and deep, abiding love begin to emerge. This is because passion and openness go hand-in-hand.

---

27. 1 John 4: 18

28. Nouwen, Henri J.M. (1990). *LifeSigns.* New York: Image Books. p.36.

Passion

Passion is often grossly misunderstood. First, it is expressed through the life of surrender, a life given to another. Passion flourishes in a life that refuses to give in to fear, but moves in freedom – the freedom of giving yourself to another. At this level of relationship the guiding questions cease to be about self, the numerous fears that hold us back are largely conquered, and newfound freedom is experienced. Passion is not something we do, but more of a driving force within. It makes its appearance in relationships as we refuse to mete out manageable parcels of our love. In the case of married love, instead of giving 15 or 50 percent of our heart to another, we pour out our own lives with no holes barred, giving 100% even if it is not always reciprocated. Central to this process is the knowledge that passionate, intimate relationships are intricately linked with God. It is in Him that we find the personal bravery to give all. If we want to experience passionate, intimate relationships we will have to reckon with the need to dispel our fears. Nouwen describes it thusly:

> Intimacy is not found on the level where fear resides. Intimacy is not a happy medium. It is a way of being in which the tension between distance and closeness is dissolved and a new horizon appears. Intimacy is beyond fear. Those who have experienced the intimacy to which Jesus invites us know that they no longer need to worry about getting too close or becoming too distant. When Jesus says: "Do not be afraid; it is I," he reveals a new space in which we can move freely without fear. This intimate space is not a fine line between distance and closeness, but a wide field of movement in which the question of whether we are close or distant is no longer the guiding question." [29]

Passion involves fervency, desire, zeal, and excitement but the root of the word is *pathos,* the word from which we derive our notion of deep feeling. Here, students of public speaking may recall Aristotle's explication of the three appeals a speaker must make to persuade an audience – *logos, ethos,* and *pathos. Pathos,* the appeal to emotion evokes the idea of shared feeling. Words such as "sympathy", "empathy," and "pathetic" all have

---

29. Ibid.

the same root, and each of them involves feeling – *shared* feeling. The feelings involved in pathos involve not only good and pleasurable emotions, but fervent, intense, feelings of grief, pain, and suffering. Yes . . . passion involves suffering. This may be hard to believe because our contemporary understanding of the word emphasizes the aspect of passion that is *desire*. Often, when the word passion is used, the first thing that comes to mind is sexual passion, and that is certainly part of the meaning. But think of the Passion story – The Passion of the Christ. The love of God expressed in the life of Jesus Christ manifested itself in the cross – an act of love and sacrifice that involved suffering, and ultimately, death. Yes, there was resurrection, and the eternal purposes of God were accomplished in the Cross, but it is important to note that true passion will include pain, long-suffering, and ultimate surrender of our self to the other, all this, because of love.

This may be easier to perceive when we discuss sexual desire, for the act of giving oneself to the other physically is an act of surrender – a giving up, a giving in, a total giving of our bodies and entire self – but in deep, intimate love relationships we will often be called upon to surrender our own particular comforts, needs and desires for the sake of the other. There are many levels of psychological, spiritual, and emotional surrender that evolve as a relationship progresses. Therein, some level of suffering takes place. As uninviting as this aspect of love may sound, it is here that true passion begins.

In spite of the sexual exploitation emphasized in the world of entertainment, what men and women long for in relationship is much more than sexual passion. People long for relationships that are full, rich, and overflowing with deep, passionate love. Because so many would-be relationships come up short, there seems to be a mad frenzy to "try people out" sexually, instead of going through the normal, much needed steps of relationship development. Each day men and women are substituting momentary physical passion for the real thing, and instead of feeling fulfilled, enriched, or *loved,* they go away lonely, broken, hurt, emotionally deformed and (after a while) even depraved . What they *really* want is a love that is true, an acceptance that is real – not performance-based – and one who will stay the subject in ongoing relationship. Tell me, what does this kind of love look like? Think: kindness, gentleness, strength, integrity, goodness, joy, self-control. Without these elements passion is reduced to a superficial (gotta-have-it) feeling.

A relationship that is based on truth has the potential to stay passionate. Without the "truth in love," passion fades. The relationship fizzles. No matter how strong the relationship may have started out, it will not last if it is not built on authenticity. But, you may ask, how can love be *genuine* if one or more of the people involved in the relationship is not genuine? Ah, a genuine person – someone who is "real." Where do we find that one? Perhaps a better question is, "How do we become that one?"

Identity

"Know thyself," the ancient Greek axiom declares. Sometimes, this is easier said than done. Understanding *who you are* has everything to do with slaying the myth that a person must find someone to complete them, and more to do with laying hold of a true sense of self. True love must emanate from a true sense of self. This matter of identity is absolutely key to developing and maintaining, strong, long-lasting, relationships. So...exactly what *is* "identity" and what is the connection between love and identity?

Identity has everything to do with individuality, and the distinctive characteristics of the *self*. While personality and character are key elements of one's identity, it has more to do with understanding *who we are*, and the answer to this question must first involve knowing *whose* we are. Be sure, taking time to understand who we are is not the same as being self-focused or selfish. Instead, it is a worthy venture, without which one may never walk confidently, with proper self-esteem.

Contemporary Western society has emphasized "the self" ad nauseam. It seems, in fact, that the axial principle "of modern culture is the expressing and remaking of 'the self' in order to achieve self-realization and self-fulfillment." [30] But taking time to focus on our identity does not mean that we saturate ourselves with endless hours of self-focus, or that we attempt to reinvent ourselves. Instead, it means that we are

---

30. Myer, Dick. (2008) *Why We Hate Us.* New York: Crown Publishers. p.66.

ready and willing to get to the root of our ability to advance in close-knit relationships. Understanding our identity is far different from giving into the stark individualism of the day. Contemporary Philosopher, Charles Taylor, speaks to this, explaining that individualism "[. . .] involves a centering on the self and a concomitant shutting out, even unawareness of the greater issues or concerns that transcend the self, be they religious, political, historical. As a consequence, life is narrowed or flattened."[31] A narrowed or flattened life is a life without love. Learning to communicate love more effectively helps to broaden our outlook, making provision for a life that is not self-focused, but centered on love.

Understanding *who we are* is important for many reasons, and concerning our subject today, it is of particular importance. This is because *who we are* forms the foundation of all of our relationships. Essentially, our identity *is* the foundation of the house of relationship. What, you may ask, does this mean? What exactly *is* the foundation of the *house* of relationship?

I like to use the metaphor of a house to describe the necessary building blocks of relationship because a relationship, more than bricks and mortar, is something in which we live. Our human sense of home is more established in the person or people to whom we have a sense of belonging than is the location or house. As with building any house, before we can talk about constructing walls, windows, or furniture, the foundation must be laid. Without a proper foundation we will try to build a "sturdy, beautiful house," only to find that when the slightest wind begins to blow – the roof caves in. With each new friend or lover we "start from scratch," and, in an attempt to reconstruct the walls or put on a new roof, we find once again that the house crumbles. Sometimes the rate at which people coming and going through our relational doors is so high that we are simply "moving the furniture around" in effort to have something new and workable. This will never do. It never works. It only leads to sadness, desperation, and loneliness. A healthy relationship is like a well-built house, one that is sturdy enough to provide a place for passion to flourish, and strong enough to withstand the storms that blow through our lives.

---

31. Taylor, Charles. (1991). *The Ethics of Authenticity.* Cambridge, MA: Harvard University Press. p. 14.

Surely, it is tempting to just slap up some walls and a roof and call it a home, but the accoutrements and outer appearance of a home do not ensure that it will be able to stand through the years. That is not how it works. The desire for a covering, a roof over our heads, a "place" (or relationship) of our own is so strong that we often rush past the necessary steps. Some of us even want to rush in and decorate — put up window treatments, plant flowers along the front porch – all before we lay the foundation. Now, pouring a foundation is not only the least glamorous part of building a house, but it's also quite time-consuming... and it is not easy work. What's more, is that long before lumber and cinderblock are purchased — even before the cement is mixed — it is necessary to get out a shovel and dig. That's right, dig. A foundation must be poured into a space that can hold it. So it is with identity. We've often got to do a bit of excavation...digging deeply within ourselves to uncover who we are.

Excavating the landscape of your soul . . . It sounds a bit esoteric, doesn't it? Perhaps even a bit daunting. Actually, it can be, but it is really nothing more than just allowing the Holy Spirit of God to come in and show you what's there. Though this may sound like it could be a fearsome task, discovering what is deep inside the ground of our being is a place we must go if we desire the fullness of true love in our lives. Yes, there might be a few worms or bugs or scary things in there... we must go... and we go with the Lord to let Him reveal to us that interior place of our soul.

Now... before we get too deep into excavation... let's explore a bit more about *why* it is so important to know who we are. How Do You Define Yourself? The Lord calls us to relationships, but we are not to define ourselves by them. When we define ourselves primarily by our relationships with others, we do a disservice to the other because:

1) We will always be looking to the other, trying to draw our sense of meaning and worth *from* the other, and

2) Ultimately, we will be more oriented to what we can *receive* from the other rather than what we can *give*.

This happens for several reasons. When we define ourselves and gain our sense of worth from our association with another person we become preoccupied with that person. Instead of simply being the most significant person in our lives, one who we love, and serve, and care for, that one begins to take on the role "need-meeter." Essentially, instead of looking at that one as a person, we begin to look to that one to meet our needs for acceptance, encouragement, affection, and companionship. Unfortunately, this does not work . . . at least not for long. Some people are able to keep up this arrangement for years, but ultimately it does not satisfy because love is more . . . much more than the meeting of our needs.

What is True Selfhood?

There is a certain patina of glamour in the colorful and creative ways individuals present their own social constructions of reality, particularly in virtual environments, or environments that exist outside of time and space. Examples of such are the social networking sites of myspace.com, Facebook and Second Life [SL].

Whether it is through an avatar in SL or a photo display on flicker, creating (or extending) one's self in cyberspace may provide several antidotes to miseries that flatten and narrow the sense of self, but do they eliminate them? Or, do they just exacerbate the problem of modernity? The diminishing sense of self that has plagued contemporary society for some time does not seem to be ebbing. Whereas television culture made deep inroads to providing the faux-finishes of self that we have come to regard as normal, Internet Culture creates new opportunities for the flourishing of self as well as the deconstruction of self. The question dangles, are these opportunities antidotes to the miseries Charles Taylor decries, or do they add to the miseries of uncertain and the human predicament?

What elements do these social constructions of self add to our lives?

- ◆   A sense of control – in a world out of control

- ◆   A way to be known – 15 minutes of fame?

- ◆   A place to belong – desire for community and intimacy

Finally, understanding "who we are" starts with an understanding of "whose we are."

Whose We Are

Once we realize that we have been made by God – created in His Image – and are known and loved by Him, we begin to grasp that *who we are* is unique. When we *know* that God is our Father and we begin to understand what is the breadth and depth and length and full measure of His love for us. . . we are changed, we are transformed. We go from constantly needy and overwhelmingly self-focused to secure . . . and much better prepared to be in a relationship of substance. That change prepares us not only to receive love from another, but to give love. And this is essential because in order to experience long and lasting love, we need to be able to give *and* to receive.

Chapter 5

Reconcilable Differences

Where is the wisdom we have lost in knowledge?

Music buffs will remember Simon and Garfunkel's blockbuster hit from the 60s, *Bridge Over Troubled Water*. It topped the charts for many months, and even if you're not a music buff, title says enough. For me, the song brings up a mental picture of the way that kind words can bring two people together even when there is trouble whirling and swirling in the waters below. Communicating love in the midst of conflict is a salve that brings healing when fellowship is broken. It is a balm that works double-duty; first, by making room for relationship to flourish, and also, by providing a path toward reconciliation, communion, and the joy of long-lasting love. Reading this, some may be thinking, "but how can I speak calmly and kindly or even think about love when I am so upset? Isn't that being dishonest?" Not at all. Communicating love always begins with considering the other before considering oneself. Even in the midst of the frustration of being misunderstood it is possible to put the other first and consider his or her feelings and needs. Relationship talk is a particular kind of communication, a mode that always involves sensitivity to the other. It must be drenched in grace and heavily sprinkled with something universally known as the *benefit of the doubt*. Yes, you've heard this before (she said with a wink), it is not new. It is the overarching positive regard for someone else that allows one individual to believe and expect that the other is being honest and means no harm. It is not rocket science, but neither is it always easy to do. Without giving others this benefit, we are apt to blurt out the most heinous accusations, most of which we truly do not even mean. A quick, thoughtless reaction usually ends up adding to the conflict.

Grace

Extending grace to the other allows us to be more careful in our response and is of utmost importance in communicating love, especially when we are in the midst of a conflict. But beyond extending grace, it is just as important to live in a *posture* of grace. Essentially, this means that we live with a built-in bias that believes in the other and makes room for them as they are — imperfections and all. Cynics may decry such an underlying attitude and advise against this, just to keep from being disappointed, but love continually looks for ways to encourage and uplift the other, and grace is the necessary ingredient that will keep relationships strong.

By now you might be asking yourself, "just what *is* grace?" Today, the meaning of grace may infer the idea of elegance or style, but it has held various meanings throughout the ages. It is a quality that bespeaks beauty, polish, and poise. A graceful person is a stable person, someone who is steady and agile. Think of a dancer, holding her position on the high bar, capable, strong, well-disciplined because she has practiced for years. In relationships, someone who is grace-full is capable of responding to another with love when conflict arises rather than reacting instinctually in defense of self. All of these character traits are reflected in loving communication, but there is much more to the meaning of grace. In the biblical sense the word means *unmerited favor*. That's right: essentially, grace is favor, or acceptance, given to another even when it is undeserved. When we walk with another in close relationship there will undoubtedly be times that we don't agree or times when one has wronged the other. Here, grace is invaluable. Without it, there is little room for forgiveness and the renewal of relationship to take place. We'll take more time to discuss this a bit later in the chapter.

In the recent past, longevity of relationship was the norm. Friends often stayed "friends for life," couples enjoyed reaching their silver and golden wedding anniversaries, and family ties were generally strong. Today, in our throw-away world where food, recreation, and basic needs are instantly available and the ease of travel makes long-distance relationships possible, the tide has changed. Many people get married *hoping* it will work out, but end up switching partners as regularly as they switch automobiles or houseplants. But people are not houseplants, and marriages need more than occasional sunshine. While there are multiple factors contributing to this trend of truncated, fractured relationships, one is at the top of the list: unresolved conflict.

Conflict. Do we need a definition? I think so. Typically, where there is conflict there is a difference of opinion, or less specifically, disagreement in the way two or more people perceive the correct way do or think about an issue. The issue may be as simple as how to do the dishes or how much maintenance a car needs. Conflict may involve lengthy dispute, simple controversy, a difference of opinion, or a sharp clash in what is perceived as acceptable behavior. It may be brought on by choosing the wrong words to express oneself, an ongoing disagreement over style or belief, or a simple facial expression or raised eyebrow. Often conflict results in a quarrel; sometimes the sad result is a broken relationship, but conflict, in and of itself, does not have to be this way. Sometimes, ongoing conflict is not so much a problem with the person with whom we are relating, but it is a matter of broken communication or, as communication scholar Paul A. Soukup explains, "a blockage." When communication is blocked, it must be fixed and it will take more than hoping or wishing your friend or spouse will forget about the conflict. It takes intentional reconciliation. To reconcile with another requires communication tools *and* the will to see conflict through to a place where the relationship is healed. Restoration of the affection, harmony, and solid relationship are the results of successful reconciliation. Soukup brings much insight to the way in which the salve of God's love can bring about healing to relationships and explains that restorative communication is like a:

> [. . .] sacred trust, motivated not by the power of one partner to dominate the other, not by the desire to monopolize the

conversation, but by the desire to let conversational partners speak what most concerns them. In this communication, we open the door for another by humbling ourselves.[32]

Humility is perhaps the most underrated element of communicating love. Without it, conflict seems to multiply like weeds in an untended garden. Even if they have been minor issues, if left unresolved they gain strength and have the capacity to undermine even the strongest relationship. Restoring the sacred trust of relationship, involves a willingness to humble oneself and make it a daily priority to stay "clean" in all relationships. What I mean by that is to keep a clean slate – a closed book on offenses. It is important to note that humility does not begin with the other person. It always begins with the individual who has a proper and healthy perception of himself or herself. Acknowledging the possibility that "I" could be wrong or that "I" may not perceive every angle of the subject at hand is a good way to start. Humility may not be the most glamorous guest at Love's table, but it must be a welcome one. A strong dose of humility is an absolute necessity in the process of resolving conflict, and it is very much a part of true love.

To walk in humility, however, there are at least three things that must never be forgotten. We must remind ourselves that:

- love is more than a feeling.

- once a relationship has developed it must be maintained.

- it is important to practice the ministry of holding one's tongue.

Love is more than a state of mind or a set of emotions that are pumped up by someone's affirmation and acceptance of us. Love is a *choice*, one that continues every single day and is strengthened by the little details in everyday life. It may not sound very romantic to think about love as a choice, but without that daily choice the romance will undoubtedly fade or fail under the pressures of life in a souped-up, 24/7 society. Some relationships seem to grow old and tired because of conflict, others because of boredom; still others cool down because the foundation of the

---

32. Soukup, Paul A., S.J. (2007). *Out of Eden*, Boston: Pauline Books p. 38.

relationship was not grounded in love itself, but in the idea or fantasy of what "being in love" means. When the illusions are swept away we are left with the other – a human being who is frail, fallen, and imperfect. There must be much more of true love in a relationship than the illusional fluff and televised versions for it to last. This we'll attend to more fully in the final chapter.

The Work of Relationship Maintenance and Reconciliation

What we have been talking about in this chapter are ways to keep our most significant relationships strong – ways to make them last. This involves what communication theorists refer to as *relationship maintenance*, a practice that cannot be managed without addressing conflict and dealing with it in life-giving ways. It is one thing to work on developing solid relationships and yet another to consider the way a relationship can be sustained. Communicating love takes time and focus. It is a lifelong process. Let's look at some very practical ways to help facilitate this process.

Consider the following words: grace, mercy, kindness, gentleness. What do they have in common? None are particularly the attributes we first think of when faced with the challenge of ongoing conflict. Yet, we must, for when conflict flares, it is the soft answer that is most likely to quell the torrent of anger. Whether friend or lover – a "kind word turns away wrath" (Proverbs 15:1). If you are the one who has been wronged, kind words and grace may be the last thing that you're in the mood to offer, but there is always a choice to make. "Will I address the problem, or leave it alone?" The answer may not be simple, however, if you want the relationship to continue, if you want your conscience to be clear, and if you would like to sleep well at night, you will choose the former. The Bible provides very practical advise in this area when Paul's reminds the Ephesians to keep their lists of offenses very short. He writes," Do not let the sun go down on your anger." (Ephesians 4: 26) Note that he does not say that there will never be anger or upset, but that we should not let even one day go by without addressing these feelings.

Conflict is not a single subject. Because it sometimes results in arguments, general upset, ongoing friction, screaming matches, or even rejection, it may seem easier to simply ignore a problem that arises in family, a friendship or a marriage; it may even seem merciful, but sooner or later that problem will resurface, even if you move on to relate to others. Therefore, when it comes to dealing with conflict, it is best to tackle it as it arises. This is especially so if "the problem" seems to be *a person*. What I mean by this is that conflict can arise from a variety of sources. The first is an actual problem or issue where there is disagreement. Another is a person whose temperament is generally disagreeable. If you are in a relationship with someone who is generally contrary, resolving conflict may become a bit more challenging, but certainly not impossible. No matter the source of it, resolving conflict requires well developed communication skills and strong character. Patience, kindness, sensitivity, and gentleness are all necessary components, but these are developed in the press of everyday life and are part of the disciplines of walking in love. What is important to remember even prior to dealing with relational issues is that conflict is *normal*. (Breathe a sigh of relief here, friends.) The good news is that conflict is not a sign that there is trouble in the relationship. People are just different: different backgrounds, worldviews, ideas, perspectives, concerns, personalities, beliefs – different. A larger problem than the conflict itself is when people ignore it or deny it in fear that it will ruin the relationship. Denying that there is conflict is a recipe for ruin. The key to conquering conflict is learning not so much how to avoid it (though this is helpful, too), but how to *deal* with it. Managing conflict is an important skill that involves grace, finesse, negotiation, thoughtful reflection and the ability to remember one thing above all, and that is – that you love this person.

Conflict tests a relationship's mettle. Will you get through it to the other side? Will hurt feelings and raw emotion be the elements that take the lead, or will forgiveness and reconciliation win out for the day? Thomas Merton explains this process of testing that occurs in every relationship. He writes:

> The purest faith has to be tested by silence in which we listen for the unexpected, in which we are open to what we do not yet know, and in which we slowly and gradually prepare for the day when we will reach out to a new level of being with God.[33]

---

33. Merton, Thomas. (1985) *Love and Living.* Mariner Books. p. 38.

Although Merton discusses the importance of waiting patiently for a new level of being with God, the same may be applied to *being with* that friend, spouse, sister or brother. True, deep, mature love takes time. Like fine wine, love gets better as it ages!

For many, it is easy to perceive the way that this love might mature and grow with a spouse or a dear friend. It doesn't just happen; over time, it grows! As we know one another, listen to one another, and walk with each other, love deepens. Henri Nouwen says it well. He writes:

> 'Time heals,' people often say. This is not true when it means that we will eventually forget the wounds inflicted on us and be able to live on as if nothing happened. That is not really healing; it is simply ignoring reality. But when the expression 'time heals' means that faithfulness in a difficult relationship can lead us to a deeper understanding of the ways we have hurt each other, then there is much truth in it. "Time heals" implies not passively waiting but actively working with our pain and trusting in the possibility of forgiveness and reconciliation."[34]

It may be more difficult to comprehend a love like this for God, but that, too, takes time to grow. Let's now take a closer look at a common challenge to these goals and seek some practical ways to communicate love in the midst of everyday life.

But She's Closed Down!

I know, I know; you say you've tried to deal with conflict in proactive, mature ways but any attempt you make to open up dialogue with her, your efforts fail. Communication is broken and you don't know how to fix it. Your friend or sister or spouse is just closed down and will not budge. Or, perhaps your brother or husband is in the ugly habit of self-justification, making excuses or rationalizing behavior that continually leads to conflict. Even the strongest communicator can experience this problem. You are not alone! This scenario can be quite frustrating. No matter how hard you try to bring restoration to the relationship, if one person

---

34. Henri Nouwen Society. *Email list word for the day.* 2009.

shuts down and pulls away there really is little hope for healing, right? Wrong. All is not lost if love can be kept alive in at least one of the members of the relationship. Surely, a loving marriage cannot be maintained if both partners do not contribute to the health of the relationship, but reconciliation and forgiveness can flow, even if it pours from one person. The power of Love is so strong that even with the most recalcitrant of lovers or friends, there is hope for change. The question is, not "if," but "where" does this hope come from? Thomas Kelly points us to the answer as he explains the completeness or perfection of love in his short book, A *Testament of Devotion* when he writes: "From our end of the relationship [we] can send out eternal love in silent, searching hope and meet each person with a background of eternal expectation and a silent, wordless prayer of love."[35] Sounds great! So where do we start? This is a good question, one that does not have a simple answer, certainly not a formula. Perhaps it is best to consider ways to make changes in our communication behavior that will be beneficial to our primary relationships.

Confrontation

There are many reasons people do not confront conflict, some of them may have little or nothing to do with carrying a grudge or offense. When a friend or spouse does not reciprocate with healing words or even the openness necessary to confront an issue, it may be a great challenge to remain loving but it is important to remember that just because someone is unable to articulate his or her feelings (or unwilling), it does not mean that he or she does not reciprocate your love. Perhaps your husband is unable to manage the pain or disappointment he feels and would rather not talk about it. Maybe your wife's coping skills are weak. Or, a friend may not want to open up that proverbial can of worms by discussing problematic issues because they fear your reaction. It could be they are unsure about their own reactions and fearful that they might not be able to control their emotions. There are many reasons why a person shuts down emotionally, and often, no matter what words you choose to help restore the relationship, the one you love

---

35. Kelly, Thomas (1996). *A Testament of Devotion* USA: HarperSanFranscisco. p. 61.

might yet remain closed. To begin bringing them back takes more than words. It will take prayer coupled with active kindnesses and attention to what they are saying both verbally and *nonverbally.*

"Look at me in the eyes" – When is the last time you heard that? Oh how we need these nonverbal cues to help us communicate what we are really feeling. As mentioned previously in our discussion of identity and intimacy, a major part of growing in our relationship is to be able to bring a full, whole self to the other, but as we each struggle to bring that healthy, whole self to the other, we must take the time to look at each other in the eyes and remind each other that we are still on the road to love – faltering on the journey, perhaps, but still walking, still seeking, still desiring to grow. One of the primary ways to communicate this is to sit down together, face-to-face, and take note of all that the other is saying, without words. Watch their body language, eye contact, gestures, and facial expressions that accompany their actions. Think before you speak. Take time to consider how they might be feeling, even if you are the one who has been wronged. Let mercy rule the day.

Confronting the other does not have to be harsh, nor should it be. However, even if strong words end up being said in haste, it is better to confront than to ignore the source of conflict. When we do, the conflict will continue to stir up the once-calm and restful waters of love and the relationship will continually exist in a state of being "at risk." Above all, do not ignore this one who seems so shut off. To ignore someone doesn't resolve the issue. Giving someone "the silent treatment" dismisses the person himself. As mentioned earlier, this kind of silence does not bring healing; it is utter rejection of the person on the receiving end. Even when the intent is not to reject, "the silent treatment" sure feels that way.

When Silence is Golden

In spite of the nemesis of the "silent treatment," a measure of silence is often needed for the restoration of a relationship. On rare occasions this silence may be necessary in the very midst of a conversation or conflict, but is most needful in learning how to wait patiently, without reacting to behavior or words that may hurt us. Like a rest in a musical score, a silent pause or "time out" from discussion can be of much help in the preservation of a relationship. There are times when pressing the pause button in the midst of a conversation is not only helpful, but necessary in order to move beyond an impasse. Loving another requires trust, and this involves so much more than matters of sexual loyalty or faithfulness. Your spouse or good friend has to be sure he can trust you with his feelings. Whether those feelings are about a particular issue or about the relationship itself, there must be an assurance that your relationship is a safe place to turn.

Pausing for a few seconds or even taking a "time-out" to cool down and reflect upon what is being said is a healthy way to utilize the option of silence. This type of silence is healing and helps us make room for one another even when we disagree. It can operate as something of a cleansing agent to bring new life to a long-term relationship. If you are still thinking of ignoring or denying the conflict, stop right now. I know you don't want your relationship to crash and burn; I don't either.

The Crash-and-Burn Syndrome

If conflict remains unresolved, disaster ensues. Not to be dramatic, but it can be just as bad as a pile up at raceway park. Emotional turmoil is no small thing. It can devastate both the relationship and the individuals involved, especially when the days begin to feel like a ride on the roller coaster at Six Flags. It is not that there is no possibility of turning back from unresolved conflict; rather that much more relational work is necessary to reestablish the close bonds of love, *and* the farther and longer you go without resolving issues, the more difficult it becomes to restore the relationship. The fact is, without the willingness to resolve conflict, relationships don't stand much of a chance of lasting. They may not end in an explosive scene, but will more likely simply fade away, limping into the sunset of what could have been life-long love. Even with the best of intentions, however, sometimes reconciliation is simply not possible, especially if the conflict has been ongoing and one person has moved on or moved away. If resolve and healing never come it may be time – probably past time – to consider getting some counseling.

The Ministry of Holding One's Tongue

When I first came upon this phrase I was surprised by the colloquial irony of it, particularly because of its origin. It comes from the writings of Dietrich Bonhoeffer, the theologian whose life was taken in a German prison camp because of the stance he took against Hitler during World War II. In his book, *Life Together*, Bonhoeffer spoke at length about the many ways the church could experience oneness and harmony in a shared life of fellowship, and addressed it in a very practical way with a daily practice he called, "the ministry of holding one's tongue," wherein silence is the most loving response to someone that is trying to cause division, or being selfish, rude or offensive. Citing the New Testament letter of James, Bonhoeffer wrote,

> It is certain that the spirit of self justification can be overcome only by the spirit of grace, nevertheless isolated thoughts of judgment can be curbed and smothered by never allowing them the right to be uttered, except as a confession of sin.[36]

Although Bonhoeffer's primary audience was a group of young seminarians, this "ministry" might easily be applied to any situation where people live in close proximity and relationship. Silence may be the most appropriate response in any relationship whether it is in a marriage, at work, in a friendship, the family, or a community of faith, while other times.

Reconciliation Through the Language of Love

The essence of love and the language used to express it contains a power that does not fade with the trends of new media or social organization. Think of it – one kind word can turn away a torrent of anger or avert gross misunderstanding. Kind words help to remind our friends, families, and spouses that we love them, but perhaps more significantly, they are an essential ingredient in the all-important process of reconciliation.

---

36. Bonheoffer, Dietrich. (1954) *Life Together: The Classic Exploration of Faith in Community.* New York: NY. p. 91.

The process of reconciling with another begins with the understanding that reconciliation is a road two people take, and even if one is more eager than the other there are definitive steps, each of which is utterly necessary. These steps may change in the order they are expressed and may be accomplished in a wide variety of ways, but minimally must include the following:

- acknowledgement of the wrong – admit it
- confession – speak it, verbally
- forgiveness – be quick to say "I forgive you"
- the reestablishing of intimacy – take time to renew and refresh the strength of relationship.

Faith, hope and love are connected

When conflicts are resolved and the relationship returns to a state of normalcy, hope returns. Everything looks brighter; friendships are mended, love is renewed, marriage is filled once again with hope and promise. It is worth taking the time to face conflict head-on and a noble task to attempt to communicate lovingly through it.

Hope is a wonderful word, but putting our faith in *hope* is an abstraction that produces little true fecundity in our relationships. True hope is tested by the kind of silence that waits patiently for an answer instead of insisting that it is instantaneous. In developing all our relationships a good measure of strength comes from waiting quietly, looking for ways to build the other up. This is faithfulness. Faithfulness is not simply refraining from disloyalty to a friend or a spouse. It is strength of relationship that creates a safety net, if you will, or an inner sanctum that provides covering from the most volatile storm. This type of faithfulness is noted in relationships throughout history and is a part of every culture, religion, and era. In Judeo-Christian tradition, the prophet Isaiah records the word of God when speaking to the people of Israel who regularly abandoned their faith in God by putting their trust in political regimes and alliances. Isaiah wrote: 'Your safety lies in ceasing to make leagues, your strength is in quiet faith." (Is. 20:15) Another translation records the prophet's words just a bit differently with the following: "Your salvation lies in conversion and tranquility, your strength in complete trust." My favorite is a much older text which reads, "In silence and hope shall your strength be." All of these translations point to the idea that faith demands "the silencing of questionable deals and strategies;"[37] it requires a type of surrender to the other that is willing to say "I love you more than my need to be right." To have faith in someone includes the ability to peaceably reconcile our differences, not always by coming to agreement; rather, reconciliation will involve a decided trust that the love is something larger and more significant than the particular issue at hand.

To separate hope and faith from a healthy relationship is impossible; the relationship – no matter how passionate or promising – will immediately fall into a state of disease, or ill-health without them. In Christian texts we are accustomed to seeing faith and hope linked with love. The three – faith, hope, and love – are intricately connected, like muscle is to the bone. While the much quoted passage from 1 Corinthians 13:13 extols love when Paul writes that "faith, hope and love abide, but the greatest of these is love," he gives the connection a bit of a different twist when he writes in verse 7, "love bears all things, believes all things, hopes all things, endures all things." The hope of the Gospel typically applies to the hope of the resurrection, but clearly, in speaking of love, Paul connects them. You may be thinking as you read, "they may be connected in Paul's mind, but how can I connect them to my relationships in everyday life?" Many people cry out with the same angst. Our busy workaday world can often confound even the greatest intention to walk in hope, faith, and love. Instead of communicating in ways that confirm our love, we often end up snapping with a reactive remark or sinking into sullenness and pouting. This is why a restorative silence is so helpful. Therein, we are able to reconnect with the truest and most noble desires, those that compel us to be patient in our hope and steadfast in our love. In his lovely explication of this connection, Thomas Merton writes: "Faith demands the integrity of inner trust which produces wholeness, unity, peace, genuine security. Here we see the creative power and fruitfulness of silence. Not only does silence give us a chance to understand ourselves better, to get a truer and more balanced perspective on our own lives in relation to the lives of others; silence makes us whole if

37. Merton, Thomas. (1985) *Love and Living.* Mariner Books. p. 38.

we let it." This sort of silence is not the same as taking time out from a heated discussion, nor is it the self-induced isolation of an introvert. Here, I am speaking of a type of silence that is actually solitude – a way of being with oneself that helps draw together the scattered energies and fragmented thoughts. It is a

> We can hope and hope and *hope* that conflict will become resolved, but unless it is combined with active faith and expressions of love, hope becomes nothing more than a stumbling block standing in the way of relationship development.

regularly practiced time that is set apart for renewal and contemplation. Silence, in this sense, can help "us to concentrate on purposes that correspond not only to the deeper needs of our own being, but also to God's intentions for us."[38] Through it, we if we allow His Holy Spirit to come and dwell we are daily renewed, both in strength and in wisdom, and our ability to communicate love will undoubtedly increase.

Communion

The integrity of a relationship stems from that inner trust in the other as someone who is genuine. Authenticity is essential. But, to have faith in a person's integrity does not mean that they will never fail or disappoint you; it does mean that you trust them and that you will give them the benefit of the doubt. As time goes on and love deepens, that faith will be tested and tried. The love is purified and transformed from merely natural affection or attraction to something touched by the Divine. This is where we have the opportunity to enter into communion with others. Communion is a very close association. It is more than simple close relationship with others; it bespeaks unity; it involves spiritual oneness. When we begin to encounter the other for who they truly are and meet them with who we truly are, we move toward a love that is so much deeper than the surface. This is communion. This may apply to both married love and love between friends or fellowship of believers. If you have never enjoyed the experience of communion in your close relationships consider it something to look forward to, a depth to which you may aspire, but take heart. All relationships start somewhere; all either progress and deepen or remain stagnant and eventually fail. Working through conflict is one way to help sustain affection and maintain, deep, long-lasting ties.

---

38. Ibid.

Resolving conflict is just part of communicating love. Another aspect of it is to be able to express the affection we feel for those we love — first in words, but also in touch. We'll take a look at the importance of touch in chapter 7. Let's now have a look at some other practical ways to communicate love in ways that create harmony, peace, and joy in our lives.

Chapter 6

Relationships on the Run

Where is the Life we have lost in living?

The convergence of media promised in the 1970s and 1980s is today a reality. The blending of print and broadcast news, the overlapping of the telephone with television and other online formats such as the Internet and wireless cellular devices — all of these media have created an environment that is highly interactive, and in many ways, refreshingly participatory. These convergent media continue to expand in everyday use, and as technologies advance we are instantly available to each other, yet the music, images, tweets and video — all these personal mobile media — compete for our attention. Sometimes managing multiple media interactions seems easy. Other times it just produces more stress, and stress is perhaps the last thing a person living in the 21st Century needs. Do you ever wonder what this may mean for our primary relationships? Some outcomes are more obvious than others. Certainly, we can stay in closer touch with our friends and other loved ones when we are not sharing the same physical space, but it also means that everyday conversations are increasingly taking place in the "in between" moments, at the same time as other activities. Typically, these pockets of time do not take place in a vacuum. There are often in the midst of public places, taking place on our way *to something else.* During these in-between moments the extraneous voices, sounds, and various other stimuli that occur simultaneously create a plethora of noise, and whether it is traffic from the street, dogs barking, a television blaring, or the details of tomorrow's department meeting sounding off *in our heads*, there is much information to be reckoned with. Whether we actually experience the stress or not, these competing noises and sounds often hinder the listener from comprehension, reflection, and thoughtful response, and they increase the level of stress for everyone involved. For example, when several conversations are taking place simultaneously (as is often the case in digital environments), the internal noise from one conversation easily bleeds into the other. Instead of coherence and meaning, there is confusion. Instead of mindfulness, there is added pressure that comes from attempting to focus in on what is being said. As you will recall, in thinking about the importance of listening, "mindfulness" is a necessary element of the process. It takes place when we focus on what is happening in the present moment. It is part of the interpretive process of listening. Mindfulness is a necessary part of the communication process that utilizes reflective listening, and is an essential ingredient in maintaining strong relationships.[39] Communicating love is hardly possible without it.

The Mobility Factor

Among the changes these new media bring, the advance and integration of our digital devices have created a shift in the way social space is shared and organized. The pace of life, in particular, has heightened. Since the industrialization of society the pace of our society has been increasing exponentially. Automobiles, air travel, fax machines, and computers, in general, have added to this increase, but the change in pace has become especially apparent since the cell phone's inception as such an immersive part of American life. Certainly, individual choices concerning use of these devices may vary somewhat, but recent statistics point to the fact that once we begin using them we easily become dependent upon them. In fact, the embeddedness of this helpful gadget reflects a trend that shows no signs of ebbing, and may reveal reasons for the increase in the daily rush and intensity of life. When surveyed

---

39. Distraction from the one purpose at hand is not isolated to relationships. In the same way, cell phone use and texting have proven unwise while driving because operating a car in traffic takes focus and mindfulness of all that is going on with drivers in surrounding lanes.

about their cell phone use, U.S. subscribers report that for 81 percent of them, the cell phone is always on. The same study reveals that 82 percent say they are irritated at least occasionally by loud cell phone users who conduct their calls in public places. While only 24 percent of cell-using adults report often feeling like they have to answer their cell phones even when it interrupts a meeting or a meal, the trend to carry on multiple conversations simultaneously seems to be increasing. Perhaps the more recent trend of text-messaging and Twitter will combat this divided focus, but, people are "tweeting" through dinner, at the movies, in the classroom, on the bus, and in church. All that to say, whether it is using our voices through cell phones and computers or our tools for writing, splitting our focus is not conducive to communicating love.

We might be tempted to think that cell phones are not much different than telephones, and that the issue is more a matter of society simply getting accustomed to a new technology. Not so. With a telephone both speakers are locatable and unable to move very far from the land line, a cell phone enables conversations to occur while on the run. Additionally, while using the telephone there is a general sense of privacy. With cell phones, privacy is often comprised because the bulk of private cell phone conversations take place in public.

When making regular use of the cell phone or the wireless Internet as a sole or primary mode of communication, it allows human beings to connect with each other at great distances, but accomplishes this in increasingly mediated fashion with extra layers of separation and space between the actual people. And, because we can do so much while on-the-go, it has become all too easy to multi-task in the midst of relationship talk, gaining a few moments to get to the next activity but losing the meaning in most of it. Meaningful dialogue is not only difficult while on-the-go, but using the cell phone to conduct important relational discussions often serves to reduce the significance of the communication taking place. Chatting like this may be workable in certain types of interpersonal relationships, particularly for the purpose of exchanging quick bits of information, but it is not sufficient to maintain primary ones, at least on a regular basis.

If this is so, what does this mean for marriages and friendships that seem to depend upon keeping current with each other through cell phone conversations, text-messages, Twitter, and Facebook? Could this type of communication behavior affect the upkeep of strong communication and self-disclosure? What about our relationships in the Body of Christ or in our nuclear families? Is the depth of our friendships and our fellowship affected by this heightened pace and advanced mobility? Does it make any discernable difference or matter at all? What do *you* think? You may want to spend some time reflecting on these ideas and take a personal look at the questions and meditations at the end of the chapter. Right now, let's explore more fully some of the ways in which our tools for communication may work in opposition to our goals for communicating love. Once found, we can work on strategies to overcome those factors that thwart our best efforts to communicate well.

Beyond Words

Easy answers and quick fixes are not possible, nor are they the goal here, but all the questions posed are important to explore, especially when it comes to our ability to sustain meaningful, intimate relationships with those we love. There is so much that our new media add to our lives that it may be easy to overlook what these digital devices take away. As media ecologist Neil Postman was long noted for saying about the incorporation of any new technology into our lives, "Technology giveth and technology taketh away." We must be aware that technology doesn't simply add something new into our lives, it changes everything! In this regard, several elements are of particular salience and stand out as most significant, such the increased pace set by these new tools of communication, the matter of social saturation, the need for affection and attention, and the cultivation of a multi-tasking mindset. Let's examine this last one first.

Multi-tasking Love

"Please give me your partial attention." Can you imagine saying that to your spouse or a friend? As a joke, perhaps, but the truth is, do any of us expect anything less than the full attention from those with whom we are in relationship? One of the most fundamental elements of love is that love requires adequate time, energy and focus.

Our multi-tasking mentality does not help this goal. The fact is, the much-lauded quality of multi-tasking is grossly misunderstood. The ability to throw clothes in a washer with a baby on your hip or preparing a meal while chatting with friends is multi-tasking. This is a far cry from attempting to explore three Internet sites while giving directions to a friend on the phone, listening to music in the background while exchanging instant messages with three other people on an open computer screen. This type of interaction with media is just that: interaction with media, not a person. Aside from the fact that relationships are not tasks on a to-do list, what this type of communication behavior leads to is something communication researchers have been calling continuous partial attention, or CPA. It is a way of being busy and interacting with one's media environment rather than relating.[40] Over time, this misuse of our media may be particularly problematic, for as we become more accustomed to giving partial attention to people, we lose the important focus necessary to truly connect and commune with others. Instead of an exception, partial attention becomes a way of life.

Along with believing that we can multi-task our relationships, several other unexpected challenges arise from our growing dependence upon personal mobile media. One of these challenges is found in dealing with the expanded reach of social influence and the increased relationship options they bring.[41] Time spent managing our social networking sites, emails, websites, discussion lists, tweets and blogs certainly afford new opportunities for connection with others, but as we embrace them our lives are apt to become overwhelmed with managing them. Now, instead of having one or two close friends and several brothers and sisters whose birthdays we like to remember, our reach has expanded to many times that amount. Kenneth Gergen, social psychologist and Swarthmore University professor refers to this as "social saturation," suggesting that this phenomenon presents a crisis in intimacy and commitment. He explains:

---

40. Continuous Partial Attention (CPA), is a phrase coined by Linda Stone in 1997. It suggests communication behavior that is "always-on" scanning, scrolling, seeking to know and be known. It has become increasingly common to live this way in the Internet generation. See *Business Week Report* July 24, 2008.

41. http://www.marshillaudio.org/resources/mp3/MHAJ-90-Reynolds.mp3 Mars Hill Audio. *Journal* Volume 90, March/April 2008 Interview with Gregory Reynolds [Retrieved June 13, 2008]

Many try to develop 'best friends' within their communities, who can be fully trusted or relied upon during a time of need. Yet it becomes difficult indeed to define a relationship as 'closest' or 'best' when for weeks, even months the participants are both in motion. Both may long for lazy and undirected hours, when each nuance of experience is examined with careful attention, and chance comments open new vistas of fascination. But consider the difficulties of locating such hours, when you take your work home with you almost every night, you know you must have more exercise, you visit your parents on the weekend, a spouse and/or children are craving for more quality time, group absorbs your Thursday evenings, and there are numerous books, games, concerts, and exhibits that are not to be missed. Under these conditions, meandering moments are seldom found, and because this is so, the very concept of 'closest' or 'best' friend undergoes a sea change. Rather than a communion of souls it becomes an occasional and compressed 'catch-up.' From a traditionalist viewpoint, we lose the capacity for genuine friendship.[42]

This sad scenario may aptly be applied to all kinds of relationships and is only rectified when we are intentional about our daily choices of interaction.

To really grasp the idea of social saturation, you might consider the image of a sponge that needs to be squeezed. It's already taken in too much water and if you keep using it, it makes more of a mess than what you started with. This is much like many of our lives: over-full, over-stimulated, *overwhelmed*. More and more people are experiencing the paltry degeneration of their primary relationships because of this situation in which too many commitments, names and dates to recall, and cultural considerations press in and overloads our lives. The countless new points of connection seem to produce more stress instead of less, and tax those most significant, primary relationships that are most cherished. While these same connections may be quite enjoyable, they ultimately reduce the time we spend relating to the most important people in our lives. I can't help thinking of one man I interviewed when studying the universe of early digital games

---

42. Gergen, Kenneth (1991). *The Saturated Self: Dilemmas of Identity in Contemporary Life*. USA: Perseus Books, P.175.

that allow individuals to simulate reality in virtual spheres. He enjoyed it because – in his words — it allowed him to escape and "sort of reinvent myself." This newlywed spent a couple of hours a day after work interacting with others through his avatar. He had so much fun relaxing with his new "friends" that some days he called in sick to work so he could spend more time in the virtual world he created online. Ultimately, he ended up spending fourteen hours a day interacting with people he would never meet, but . . . it was fun. Within a year his job was gone and so was his wife.

> **Think on these things....**
>
> "Whatever is true, whatever is lovely, whatever is excellent and pure, think on these things," wrote St. Paul to the young Philippian church. (Phil 4:8). When we fill our mind with that which is good and worthy of praise, it is much more likely that we will communicate in ways that reflect this goodness. Try it for one solid day. Each time your thoughts gravitate toward complaint, grudge, anger, or rage, take a breath. Stop, and begin to list the things for which you are thankful. Dwell on what is good, noble, and pure, and watch your communication style change for the better. You will be taking one more step toward more effectively and graciously communicating love.

Another example of our problematic propensity to multi-task lies in the arena of public civility. In some ways, fascination with our media cuts us off from the thicker context of relationships all around us and increasingly diminishes civility. Whether at home or in public places, if our eyes are fixed on a screen we lessen our possibilities of interacting with others more informally, people we might meet in the public square, on the bus, or in the supermarket line. As we think about communicating love, it is certainly in the context of our primary relationships, but should we not go further and consider our neighbor? The individual sitting in the waiting room may be a stranger, but she is a person, too. As we close ourselves up in our communication tools we create a bubble around us that disassociates us from other human beings, shutting us off from the potential of knowing them, or at the very least, treating them as an individual rather than an object.

In the midst of this shift in social behavior, it is important to remember that it is not the technological changes or the particular medium itself that is to blame. While Technology's tools are far from neutral instruments, they are also inanimate and cannot "do" something outside of human use. Neither is it solely the content shared through these media that are such a mighty influence. Essentially, it is not even what we do with them in singular situations which are the most significant factors in effectuating change. Rather, it is *most* important to recognize how these new technologies reorganize human relationships and, in doing so, redefine for us what things we value, and what things we do not. The history of technological advance suggests this time and again. From the horse and buggy to the automobile, and the radio to the television, in hindsight we see clearly how they have changed the social landscape in our world. As we use our personal mobile media it is important to see that in the same way, they are reshaping our communities, families, and lives as a whole. Thankfully, there is no one forcing us to use our digital devices ways that are destructive to our personal relationships, but with each new application and advance in software it seems we must be more intentional about keeping them from using us.

Earlier I mentioned that communicating love takes more than words. You know it; I know it; there is not a soul in relationship who does not understand the way nonverbal communication affects our ability to stay strong and connected. Our actions must correspond to the words we use, but try as we might, sometimes there is a disconnect! Sometimes the very best of intentions do not lead to successful expression. Learning to demonstrate our love through actions and expressions is a lifelong process, and part of that process must include learning to communicate our love through touch.

Touch communicates love and tenderness in ways that are far beyond words. From a hug to a handshake or a gentle pat on the back, our bodies respond to touch perhaps more quickly and dramatically than any other means of nonverbal communication. Learning how to express our feelings appropriately and sensitively through the human touch is most certainly a worthwhile endeavor. So let's go there now. Let's take a look at some of the ways affection and love are connected and explore the beauty of the physical body.

Chapter 7

Close Encounters

Where is the knowledge we have lost in information?

My dear friend was crying today over a broken dream. It was something that she cherished in her heart for many years and finally she just had to let it go. Where was I as the tears trickled down her face? I was online; *there,* but *not really.* I looked at her email with a wince and sat there, staring at a cold blue screen, reading her misery, relating to it all too well. Although I immediately responded to her message – and she was somewhat comforted – what my friend needed was a hug.

How easy it is to forget that we really need is the affirmation and comfort of physical presence. We are living in an era when so much of the material world competes for our time and attention. It is easy to conclude that once our relationships are established they can just take care of themselves, or, that the virtual life is "just as good" as being there. Neither of these options is grounded in reality. We can contact friends via email, send quick, witty messages via text, and even enjoy receiving photos of events happening clear across the world in moments — and surely it is *better than nothing.* But, after a while the substitution of screen life for physical reality begins to wear even the most closely-knit relationships. Others, operating on the assumption that sending messages to each other is enough to maintain close relationships, only find disappointment and heartache. So many people who experience breakups are bewildered about how such strong relationships could be thwarted, but increasingly it is clear that it is in the everyday interactions that communication breakdown begins.

Knowing that your friend or spouse is *with* you is a salve and balm for which there is no substitute. In fact, much of the dysfunction and confusion in our friendships and marriages may emerge more as a result of the need to be touched or affirmed than they do from actual problems. If your friend, child or spouse seems to need an unending supply of compliments and recognition, the root of the problem may find its root in the need for affection. So often we find ourselves striving to be recognized, sending out messages that scream, "See me," "Notice me," "Pay attention to *me!*" when what is actually needed is simple affirmation. An affirming word, nod, or gentle touch can bring healing and satisfaction because it addresses *who we are* as opposed to *what we do*, or what we may accomplish. This should come to no surprise for we are human *beings*, not human *doings*; yet we can become so accustomed to working hard, pressing forward with our daily responsibilities, and communicating through layers of media that we are apt to forget the most basic essentials of life. The foremost of these is the incomparable value found in our closest relationships, and perhaps the most important aspect of which is remembering that being in relationship means nothing less than *being with* one another. *With-ness,* for want of a more explicit term, is something we just can't skimp on. While we are most certainly spiritual beings with emotions, desires, deep thoughts, and an eternal destination, we are also bodies; that is, people who are *physical* — made in the image and likeness of God. We are *persons,* made to function in the midst of the mystery and marvel of creation. Being made in God's image privileges human beings with certain advantages and responsibilities, and this *imago dei* affects our capacity for relationship in numerous ways. In this chapter, we will continue to explore this foundational aspect of interpersonal communication, along with the importance of being *fully* present to one another. Then we will take a deeper look into how each of these elements is absolutely key to helping our closest, most significant relationships stay on course.

Physicality

The human body is an amazing, fragile, resilient, and complex organism, full of dichotomies, tensions, reflexes, needs, capabilities, and desires. To say that our physical bodies are important is an understatement, but they are certainly much more than just mere containers that house our souls, as some would suggest. We have been fearfully and *wonderfully* made! In spite of our inherent frailties and the obvious limitations of our physicality, our bodies are not to be despised, forsaken or downgraded to something less than what they are. They are not to be overlooked. Yet, they are not to be idolized, either. Our bodies are the work of a Master; they are to be cherished, appreciated and treated with respect, *even awe*. Is this a little bit overboard? I don't think so. Consider for a moment the incarnation of Christ. Here, the Great Holy Spirit and Creator of the Universe deemed physical presence important enough to send His Son to live in the midst of the human race at a particular point situated in time and space. Although the Word is living and active, speaking to us today, the incarnation of Christ gives great weight to the importance of embodiment, for it was on the earth in a physical body that the son of God lived, breathed, and walked among us. It was here that he was crucified, died, buried, and here that He rose again. It was to human flesh that the Lord revealed Himself, inviting humanity to once again live in unbroken fellowship with our Creator. In her lovely book, *Sacred Rhythms*, Ruth Haley Barton confirms this:

> All the great themes of scripture affirm the significance of the body as a place where the presence of God can be known and experienced. The incarnation itself – Christ's choice to take on flesh and inhabit a human body – forever elevates the experience of embodiment to the heights of spiritual significance.[43]

Beyond the immeasurable worth of the redemption is the relational significance of the incarnation. The embodiment of God's Word in Christ teaches us many things, one of which is that love must be practiced and lived out in relationship. Relationship is established and expands amidst all the suffering, pain, joy, and exultation of actual physical presence. It is not esoteric. Rather, love is situated firmly in the body.

---

43. Haley Burton, Ruth. (2006). *Sacred Rhythms*. Downers Grove, IL: Intervarsity Press. p. 81.

Love is more than talking about it.

Love is more than a feeling.

Love is more (much more) than an abstraction.

To know if we truly love someone or if we are truly loved we need to take love out of the abstract, virtual sphere and into real life. In our closest physical relationships, that is, the covenant between husband and wife, it is perhaps the easiest to perceive.

Consider, as well, the intricate design of all that is in the world, the exquisite union and delight of sexual intimacy between a husband and wife to the mystery and grandeur of childbirth. These wonders are grounded in the inexplicable mystery of love, a love that finds its most intimate expression in the bodily coming together of two human beings who have taken the time to really know each other and can flourish further by translating the emotional, intellectual and psychological knowledge to the marriage bed. This deep affection expressed by husband and wife is part of a life together – a life of celebration. It is therefore, "not one in which two people seek to love each other in spirit and truth in spite of their bodies, but on the contrary, use all resources of body, mind, heart, imagination, emotion, and will in order to celebrate the love that has been given them by God, and in so doing to praise Him."[44]

Inside the marriage relationship, the affection and love associated with sexual union is not just a good idea, it is something to be cherished. One of the worse comic sketches I ever heard involved a joke about marriage. In a mocking tone the comedian bantered about what it is like to be middle-aged and married and said something like, "you know it, men; it's all argument and no sex." Ugh. No. That need not be so. Married couples need to keep active sex lives – healthy sex lives – giving to one another liberally and without holding back, receiving from one another with gratefulness and joy. Sexual union is just part of this picture, and an important one, at that, but there is much more to the need for physical presence in marriage. The most significant one that comes to mind is the need to give and receive affection – the gentle touch, the loving look, the tender tone of voice. Now, amidst the ringing

---

44. Merton, Thomas. *Love and Living.* P. 105.

choruses of "amen," I can almost hear a few of you dismiss that last sentence as perhaps pertaining to other people, but not applicable to you. You may be thinking, "Not me. I don't come from a demonstrative family," or "We never made much of affection growing up – love is much more than that!" Come now, don't be too quick to ignore what countless happily married couples have found to be true: affection is necessary everyday. It is the glue that keeps the love strong and healthy. Affection shouts in the face of our workaday world that love is the foundation of our relationships, that there is more to life than efficiency and getting things done; it is the tangible reminder that love is the cornerstone of the relationship.

Aside from sexual union in the marriage covenant, the significance of bodily presence in our relationships is profound on many levels. The look in someone's eyes, the soft or tender voice – all are necessary. Our bodies can survive on beans and rice for months, but there are detrimental affects to going without a well-balanced diet. The same is true for our psychological well-being. Our bodies are capable of functioning without affection, but it is to the detriment of our souls. The flourishing of our souls is not just a good idea; it is essential. Fecundity is part of the plan and purpose of all creation. We may be able to survive a terrible breakup or get along well enough to stay married, but a love that flourishes is part of the pattern and promise of life itself. This fecundity will not be evidenced without paying attention to the need for affection.

Deep Affection

If you are of a certain age you will likely remember the lanky, freckle-faced Alfalfa of early television's *The Little Rascal's*. What a crush that boy had on a glamorous little girl named Darla. I can still hear his squeaky adolescent voice croak out the song that was directed specifically at her: *"The object of my affection, can turn my complexion from pink to rosy red...."* Do you remember it? Feelings of affection have a way of creeping up on a person, and, despite all efforts to be cool and calm, these feelings can be explosive and seemingly uncontrollable. Yet, affection does not mean quite the same thing for everyone. Neither is it synonymous with sexual union or arousal. The word affection comes from the Latin *affectio*, an emotion of the mind, but like so many other words, its meaning has morphed throughout the ages. Today, affection may still mean that special feeling of tenderness and closeness one has for another, but the word is more often associated with outward displays of love, especially, touch. Affection includes both touch and other appropriate expressions of caring. It is not just kisses and hugs. The benefits of affection are more obvious to our relationships than the need for affection. Often, it seems, the need to give and receive affection is misunderstood. However, while these benefits are immense, they are grossly underrated. C.S. Lewis reminds us of the need when he wrote that "Affection is responsible for nine-tenths of whatever solid and durable happiness there is in our lives." That's quite a statement, and quite a bit of happiness! Happiness is an abstract state of being which surely means different things to different people, but the universality of it makes it important to apply Lewis' words to our own lives and relationships with vigor. Consider the fact that our skin is our largest organ, weighing about six pounds and containing countless nerve endings. *They aren't all there for the benefit of sexual intimacy.* We need affection!

The need for physical affection has been documented through many studies, particularly regarding infants who have been deprived of human touch. Lynda Harrison, a researcher in the School of Nursing at the University of Alabama at Birmingham explains the effect lack of touch has on babies that are born prematurely, saying: "We know that many of the babies who were put into orphanages in Europe after World War II developed what we call 'failure to thrive.' They received calories, but they were not nourished with parental touch. They did not grow, and many developed severe social problems."[45] For babies, the benefit of physical contact is a matter of life and death,[46] but the need for physical contact is important for all ages and may especially as it is applied to the quest for deeper, more significant close relationships.

To benefit a relationship, all types of affection must be demonstrated, not just kept tidily hidden deep in one's heart. Bringing a friend a meal or your spouse a cup of tea; greeting your daughter with a loving look and smile, making eye contact with your dad; all these measures are means of demonstrating affection.

---

45. Shuler, Roger, "*Techniques of Touch: New Knowledge about Nurturing Newborns*" *UAB Magazine,* Summer 2001 (Volume 21, Number 2). University of Alabama at Birmingham Press.

So, if you feel warmly affectionate toward your friend, why not show her? Did you think of her this morning kindly or in prayer? Perhaps a quick note or phone call to say hello and "I was thinking of you" is in order. How important it is to show affection to the ones we love. It is a prime way of communicating love. If you feel loving toward your spouse it is essential to express it. Stop and give her a hug on the way out the door, even if her hands are in dishwater! Put the book down for a moment and give your husband a quick kiss to say hello (or maybe not so quick!)

Once we subject ourselves to the pace of life it becomes increasingly easier to neglect the simple demonstrations of love. Once this occurs it becomes much easier to fall into the habit of not expressing the affection we feel at all. Countless divorces and broken relationships are the result of this type of relational neglect. It never ceases to amaze me each time I hear a man or a woman claim that their divorce came "out of the blue," or that they still love each other but cannot manage to get along. Often, that type of brokenness is a direct result of neglect in the area of affection. No matter how strongly we feel love for a person, if that affection is unexpressed it does no one any good at all. All of our best intentions cannot make up for the lack of love's expression, but just as in our conversations, there are many things that get in the way of giving and receiving affection. Everyday distractions are just a part of the hindrances. Busyness, uncertainty, and even fear can inhibit our ability to give *or receive* affection.

For many people, it is much more comfortable to allow a screen to mediate our relationships, but a screen – no matter the size – is very similar to a wall. We may be able to communicate with ease on the virtual plane, but we do not benefit from keeping walls between us. Without face-to-face contact it is difficult to develop the trust necessary to sustain our relationships. We need to be in each other's presence.[47] Along with affection and trust,

---

47. Recent research in neuroscience points to the efficacy of the face in building trust. Dr. Damasio has studied faces in which large number of faces of men and women without particular facial expressions in which a large number of people were asked to rank the faces according to how much they might trust this face? People's faces were divided into five categories. Some inspired trust extremely. Damasio, a Professor of NeuroScience at University of Southern California, asks: What happens in our brains to cause us to trust people? The overarching finding is that we need the human face to develop trust. *Talk of the Nation* radio program. July 24th, 2009. "*How Does the Brain Decide Who to Trust?*" National Public Radio.

face-to-face communication allows us to go beyond the surface. This is not only essential in terms of necessary communication cues, such as eye contact and facial expressions, but it helps our relationships to gain greater breadth and depth, leading to greater levels of intimacy. Without face-to-face communication we give up the promise of true dialogue and end up communicating with others in bits and bytes – fragments, phrases, and acronyms rather than full sentences pregnant with feeling and meaning. In many ways we have become a sound bite society. This is especially so with the entrance of Twitter. Yes, mediated relationship *is* convenient, but – again — have we asked ourselves, 'what have we lost?' We know what we have gained, but technology is never neutral; there is always a give-and- take. To be wise in our use of these media we must remember this and ask ourselves, 'what is the exchange rate?' What does the added convenience of these media do to the depth and richness of our relationships?

These questions will always be important, for as soon as new media become pervasive they become largely invisible. Once these media become embedded in our everyday lives and our senses acclimate to the changes that take place, awareness of their reorganizing vitality fades. For this reason I regularly conduct a study with students to help them (and all of us) remain aware of how our media choices are affecting our relationships and perception of reality. In one particular part of the research I spent seven years asking individuals between the ages of 16 and 29 to share their perceptions and experiences of relationship conducted via new media. Nearly all of the over 500 participants noted how the quality of their relationships had become more sparse since conducting so much of their social lives through cell phones, text messages, and computer screens. Despite the sheer enjoyment of these communication devices, the highest percentage of all participants said these media also served to distract, water-down, and fragment the relationships they held most dear. So, in spite of having more information, access, *and* interaction with others, the findings clearly demonstrated a qualitative difference between information and knowledge. It brings us back to the questions T.S. Eliot raised his poetry in the mid-20th century:

Where is the Life we have lost in living?

Where is the wisdom we have lost in knowledge?

Where is the knowledge we have lost in information?[48]

The major difference between knowing a great deal about a person and being close with a person is the difference between information and knowledge. Close friendship, as with any type of love, means, necessarily, that people will spend time together, in each other's presence, learning from each other, growing in the experience of the other. As much as we are living in the Age of Information, it is not possible to know another (or be fully known) through facts. We do not learn about the depths of our friend's soul by asking him to fill out a list of twenty-five facts about himself. There is mystery in this process accompanied by much excitement and joy as we grow more deeply in love with others. The mystery is not necessarily to be conquered, but it is to be respected and acknowledged. To know the other, we must experience that one. In the same way that we can memorize every jot and bit of information about human anatomy and the reproductive system, and still be confounded and amazed by the birth of a little baby, we can carry around a great deal of information about a person and still not really know him. Knowledge is different than information; it is beyond the surface; it is deep. Getting to know someone requires knowledge of their soul – their interior. For relationships to remain intact and close we must be willing to go deeper with one another and, among other things, that means acknowledging the whole person, accepting who they are, and remain willing to spend time together. Once we respect and honor the need for physical presence, the way has been made clear go deeper.

The Sexiest Part of the Human Body

Once, at an academic conference in Mexico City, I heard a presentation by Frank X. Dance, a noted communication scholar who has spent years doing research investigating the physiology of communication. Dr. Dance stated that the human voice was the sexiest part of the human body and woke us all up! *Hmmm.* Could that be true? I am not sure, but I do know that the human voice may be the most powerful agent in making meaning and intimacy, for there is still nothing as perfect as the sound of the

---

48. Eliot, T. S. Choruses from "*The Rock.*" *Collected Poems,* 1909-1935. New York: Harcourt, Brace, c. 1936. 179.

human voice calling from inside one person to the inside of the other. The power in it is visceral. The relationship between experiencing someone's presence and the world of sound has been brought to bear by many philosophers, but Walter J. Ong captured it well in an anecdote he shared about the hunter and the buffalo when he said:

> The hunter, remember, can see, touch, smell, and taste a buffalo when the buffalo is inert, even dead. If he hears a buffalo, it's a different matter: the buffalo is doing something. *Sound signals the present use of power.* Scholars sometimes say that primitive peoples naively associate words with power. It is such scholars who are naïve: if you think of real words, of sounds, words are always an indication of power-in-use.[49]

With the exception (perhaps) of touch, the power of the human voice to demonstrate affection is unsurpassed. Sound comes from within an individual reaching out to the interior of another. As our voices connect with one another through conversation, they do so in much deeper ways than writing or text message. Although a letter can be very personal, writing is external and much more formal. Ong explains further, "even in the physical world this is so. Sounds echo and resonate, provided that reciprocating physical interiors are at hand. Sight may reflect from surfaces."[50] Think about that for a moment, now. What is needed for resonance is *reciprocating physical interiors.*

Deep Calling unto Deep

"Deep calls to deep at the sound of your waterfall."

Although sexual union between a husband and wife is a gift that brings the couple into even greater intimacy, without the willingness to communicate from one heart to another, there is no resonance, and no matter how frequently the two engage in physical union, there will be no true intimacy. In order to move toward true intimacy with one another we must push past the exploitative roles popular culture tempts us to play and seek to know the other in truth. For

---

49. Altree, Wayne. (1973). *Why talk? A conversation about language with Walter J. Ong.* San Francisco: Chandler and Sharp Publishers. p. 15.

50. Ong, Walter *The Presence of the Word,* p. 125. [emphasis mine]

this we do not need thousands of dollars in counseling or expensive adventures on land or on sea, but we do need to be in each other's physical presence, and we do need to actually *hear* one another. This is partially because "of its very nature, the sound world has a depth, dimension, fullness such as the visual, despite its own distinctive beauties, can never achieve."[51] Yet, here we are, in a world where the sound of one's voice and physical presence are no longer as necessary as they once were. It is a world where mediated conversations are the norm, a world where the image is king. It is a situation where we are living, working, and relating in the midst of a media landscape that is laden with images, and we are acculturated to this world of vision where "seeing is believing." The very commonness of this phrase reveals its veracity, and the fact is, over half of our cerebral cortex is dedicated to interpreting visual images. One may say that we are hard-wired for interpreting images. Yet, images are appearances of deeper realities. Jus as there is much more to every person than their appearance – always, there is more than meets the eye. If we hope to get to know those we care about and maintain deep, life-long relationships we must not give in to the notion that we can satisfying ourselves with only the external. Seeking to know someone beyond the outer layer of external attractiveness is challenging. It is even counter-cultural. Yet, it is the most worthwhile adventure in all of life. We'll discuss this in greater depth in a few minutes. Right now, let's dig deeper into the reasons we are so prone to substitute really being with another with watching TV or a movie together.

Entertaining versus Relating

From the very start of a person's life the need for physical affection is prominent and must be fulfilled. It sets the course for healthy self-perception and socialization, and certainly, helps to secure the probability for strong relationships in the future. Yet, so much of what is projected on screens, especially in the developmental stages of life (from birth – 12 years old) makes an imprint on our brains that creates neural pathways – essentially, a brain bias – to learn and remember that which is gleaned from visual stimuli. From

---

51. Ong, Walter. (1981). *The Presence of the Word: Some prolegomena for cultural and religious history*. Minneapolis: Minnesota University Press. p. 125.

billboards and magazines to televisions, computers and screens from mini to mammoth, human perception in these postmodern times is largely trained through sight. Raised in a world of print we begin to lay hold of reality through words on a page. From the earliest stages babies now learn through the visual medium of television, DVDs and computers. Growing up with Bert, Ernie, and Oscar the Grouch as our daily companions we learn to laugh and find joy in being entertained rather than related to. As parents, we may be inclined to take offense at such implications because it is "educational programming," but that doesn't change the way learning takes place. Children learn to phase out the desire for affection if it is not maintained as normal and natural, filling the gap with a myriad of other comforts from drugs and premarital sex to all manner of anti-social and dysfunctional behavior that they have watched on screens since they were very small.

Exploitation

In some ways the need to emphasize the importance of physically expressing our love may seem counter-intuitive, especially when considering the manner in which the human body has been idolized and exploited in popular culture. But instead of conceiving of the body as something to be respected, enjoyed and loved, it is increasingly portrayed as something to be used. This exploitation has expanded to something nearly all-encompassing. From the songs we sing and entertainment we consume into our collective consciousness, the body has been relegated to something primarily fixated on the sexual act or associated with sexuality, in general. Because of this, it is easy to perceive the body as an object – something that is either grossly impure and unworthy, or lopsidedly significant –a *thing*, to be used and discarded as whim or feelings lead. This lowly status of the human body does not negate the need for affection, but often eclipses the need for emotional support and care of the individual as a whole. Thomas Merton expands upon this idea suggesting that it has resulted in a filthy and dreadful atomization of love, and explains what this kind of thinking about love does.

> [It] puts the human body on the market, either as a desirable package of commodities and pleasures or as a highly

dangerous compound of moral evil. Love becomes no longer an expression of the communion between persons but a smorgasbord of the senses in which one selects what he wants – or what he thinks he can get away with. [52]

To be sure, the relational benefits of giving and receiving affection have much farther reach than the drive for sexual intimacy. When empirical studies have been conducted in the fields of psychology, communication, and cognitive brain science, all point to the same conclusions: that there are psychological and emotional benefits of affection as well as the healing benefits of touch. One study, found that "the amount of affection participants received from their fathers during their upbringing was inversely associated with their likelihood of suffering clinical depression." [53] Kory Floyd, the Arizona State University communication professor whose research in the area of affection between the sexes, in friendship, and in parent-child relationships has spanned several decades, explains that although no direct causal inferences can be made, all the studies point in similar directions. He explains, "In all instances, the amount of verbal, direct nonverbal, and support-based affectionate communication characterizing the relationships was directly associated with such outcome measures as relational closeness, liking and love, relationship satisfaction and communication satisfaction."[54] In fact, in studies that measured happiness, fulfillment, and relational satisfaction with the amount of affection evidenced in the relationship, Floyd and his co-authors consistently found that the "more affectionate people were, the happier, more socially active, less stressed, less depressed, and more satisfied with their romantic relationships they were."[55]

To experience affection and benefit from it on a regular basis, we need to actually *be* with each other. Again, we are back to *with-ness*. There is just no substitute for it. Consider this: what does it mean to "be there for" a person, if not in physical proximity? While it is true that we can be "with" one another in spirit, or "with" one another in a decision about where to go for vacation or what

---

52. Merton, Thomas. *Love and Living*. p. 100.

53. Floyd, Kory *Communicating Affection*. Canbridge University Press, 2006. p. 89.

54. Ibid.

55. p 95, Ibid

to have for dinner, unless we are spending time actually sharing the same physical space, our ability to communicate love is greatly hindered. Being with a person "in spirit" doesn't help much if they need a ride to the airport or a dinner companion. Tender, consistent affection is an important aspect of the physical means of communicating love to others. It is part of the way we nurture intimacy, but there are many other ways, as well.

Intimacy and True Presence

We discussed intimacy a bit back in chapter three, but love, as the song goes, is a many splendored thing, and the subject of intimacy warrants further discussion. Whereas relationships are built on being with each other, in each other's presence, intimacy grows as we are *fully* present to the other. Being fully present means a great deal more than just being in the same room. It means attending to the other, as other. Knowing the other *as other* is a phrase introduced by Martin Buber in the mid-20th century. A philosopher and theologian, Buber stressed the importance of approaching the other as a fully human subject. This, he emphasized, is directly opposed to approaching that one as an "it," or *an object*. It may sound a bit odd to think that grown adults could confuse people with things, but many of us do it every day and are conditioned to do so through modern, post-industrial communication techniques, such as advertising, public relations, and the mass media.

To be fully present to one another is a gift that we can give the ones we love, a gift that does not cost a penny, but is surely priceless. One aspect of this is what communication researchers, Kenneth Cissna and Rob Anderson have referred to as immediacy of presence which simply means to be available and "relatively uninterested in orchestrating specific outcomes or consequences. Immediacy of presence suggests both the 'now' and the 'here' dimensions of communication. *Now* recognizes that the present is neither past nor future, whereas *here* notes presence as a placement in space."[56] This type of immediacy has as much to do with attention as it does physicality. Whereas to be with a person means to be in

---

56. Anderson, R., Cissna, K,, and Arnett, R. Annett, (1994). *The reach of dialogue.* Creskill, NJ: Hampton Press, pp. 13-14.

the same general proximity, being fully present is more about the kind of focus we bring to that one. Being fully present to another means that we present ourselves to each other in a place where eyes can meet, hands can touch, and one interior meets with another, for "Presence is not what is evanescent and passes, but what confronts us, waiting and enduring."[57]

Along with the need to actually be in someone's physical presence, we must reckon with the person in front of us, not the one we imagine him to be. The friend we know who may have behaved poorly last week or the person who may disappoint us again next week does not exist. It is in the moment that we may relate to that friend or spouse. Yes, what happened in the past *was* real, but we do not have a past other to confront and if we relate to the other from any other position but the present, we are apt to project our ideas and judgments upon them rather than receive them for who they actually are. Whether a disappointment or an exultation – the past was real, but life is constantly changing and so is every living being. We have the one who confronts us now – today – in our presence. Without appreciating and apprehending the friend who today looks me in the eye and is present, we run the risk of reducing that one to an object – an *it* – rather than a person. We are inclined to relate to that one in a way that is less than respectful, depersonalizing him or her as part of the world of things. This is a common result of what happens when we buy into the media-driven ideas of the other. Saturated in the images and ideas purported by advertising campaigns and reality TV, it is all to easy to begin to "consider ourselves and others not as persons, but as products – as 'goods,' or in other words, as packages. We size each other up and make deals with a view to our own profit."[58] It is nearly impossible to communicate love and cultivate intimate relationships when we view ourselves and others this way, particularly if much of our communication takes place digitally.

Particularly today, in the current media environment where personal mobile media such as Internet-capable cell phones are being used with increased frequency to exchange messages via text, the experience of being fully present to one another is losing out.

---

57. Buber, Martin. (1970). *I and thou.* In Walter Kaufmann (trans.). New York: Scribner. p. 44.

58. Merton, Thomas. In *The reach of dialogue*, 1994. Anderson, Cissna, and Arnett (1994). Creskill, NJ: Hampton Press. P. 251.

Unthinkingly, many of us may enjoy the greater convenience and speed that these devices allow while not realizing the potential they have to weaken our most important relationships. Perhaps the most significant way this happens is that they lessen the opportunity for face-to-face interaction where thoughtful, focused conversations can take place. Instead of taking time to investigate a potential problem or misunderstanding, conversation is often reduced to soundbites — fragments of information rather than deep sharing. When our communication with others is reduced to this we inadvertently trade the integrity and responsibility of deeply knowing and caring for others into depersonalization. In particular, our friends and families are continually at risk of objectification. The depersonalizing effects of communicating through mediated means seems to be nipping at the heels of all relationships.

Encounter

Uncovering the mystique of the unknown "other" is very much a part of the reason human beings use language. There is a certain ineffable quality consistent in being with the other that a computer screen or virtual environment cannot simulate. Encounter is part of the mystery of life. It is part of the mystery that makes love an incontrovertible and universal drive. The word *encounter* primarily means to meet someone, or come upon him in passing, but as Martin Buber used the word it came to mean much more, encompassing the need for truly knowing others as subjects, as actual persons. This type of knowing, or *encounter*, infers the type of relationship that close friends, family, and couples surely desire.

Language helps us to "get to know the other," mediating the distance between one person and the other. The overwhelming delight of this interplay is brought to bear through the countless tales of relationships as they are told and retold in some of the greatest works of fiction in history and portrayed in film and television. In fact, it may be said that observing relationships is a national pastime. As personal mobile media gain greater breadth throughout society and relationships boundaries are increasingly carried into the streets, the workplace, beaches, parks, and airplanes, it may also appear that the value of relationship has increased. From the online dating services and homemade wedding videos on YouTube, to tales of friends and lovers being reunited through the Internet, stories of new romantic connections seem to confirm the emergence of a whole new world of .[59] Chatting on the way to work, texting while in meetings, or connecting through Facebook — people are talking! New media *do* create a plethora of new opportunities to use language in creative ways, but these wireless technologies have changed the ways in which we relate to each other in that the ever-presence and ease of accessibility create a magnified familiarity, a hyper-knowing of others. In one way, they seem to take the mystery out of relationship. Joshua Meyrowitz (1985) confirms this in his findings in research with prior technologies, where he discussed the relational ramifications of television. In spite of the different type of media an overlapping and quite cogent application to newer electronic media exists. He wrote,

> If the mystery and mystification disappear, so do the formal behaviors. Stylized courtship behaviors, for example, must quickly fade in the day-to-day intimacy of marriage. Similarly, the new access we gain to distant events and to the gestures and actions of the other sex, our elders, and authorities does not simply "educate" us; such access changes social reality.[60]

Cultural conception of love and marriage changed in major ways through the pervasiveness of television, and the same is happening with our new media. While there are always the exceptions, all of these increased opportunities to participate in relationship may be on the upswing but the depth and solvency of relationship seem to be fading. They are increasingly fragmented and partial. The hyper-familiarity of status updates on facebook or a hourly tweets seem to steal some of the power out of a sound and solid conversation. So, relationships are changing, times are changing, and as the old phrase suggests, maybe we just need to "get with the times!" But, maybe not. We can use our tools of technology to help us communicate, but that does not mean that the heart of relationship has changed or the universal need for love and affection. There are many aspects of relationship that remain exactly the same as they have for ages. We may court via text

---

59. An example of this in popular culture is found in the portrayal of relationship development through e-mail in the 1998 film *You've Got Mail* in which Joe Fox (Tom Hanks) and Kathleen Kelly (Meg Ryan) fell in love with each other through daily e-mail exchange.

60. Meyrowitz, Joshua. (1985). *No sense of place.* New York: Oxford University Press. p. 309.

instead of riding in cars or taking long romantic walks on the beach, but the longing for true love remains the same. Friendships may be conducted increasingly through long distance communication, but true love is still among the most cherished and longed for relationships in everyday life.

Relationshipping

Friendships are not singular events strung together over the course of a few months, and marriage is not the sum of Friday night movie dates and special anniversary celebrations. Family is more than yearly birthday cakes or trips to the zoo. These close relationships build, over time, and they build through shared experiences, conversation, and spending time together. Many people don't consider themselves "good" at relationships, which is sometimes a matter of perception and other times simply the truth. The good news is that relationship skills can be appropriated and advanced. Relationships are part of the process of communication, and very much threaded through everyday life. Interpersonal communication researcher Steven Duck describes the process as "relationshipping," and speaks of it as a something one can learn, saying: "Because it is a skill, relationshipping . . . is something that can be improved, refined, polished (even coached and practiced) like any other skill, trained like any other, and made more fluent."[61] However, this sophisticated, complex process of relationshipping requires greater attention, focus, and intentionality than we are often willing to give it, and, perhaps more than any other factor, it requires time. Relationships take time to grow.

To communicate involves a process that allows people access to one another – a process in which people engage in meaningful discourse and a way to gain greater understanding of each other and essentially, of what it means to be human. More than literature, film, or any other mode of telling the human story, face-to-face communication is that part of the symbolic exchange that helps to provide equipment for living, enabling people to know and relate to one another.[62] Communication is not simply a matter of

61. Duck, Stephen. (2006). *Our friends, ourselves.* In Stewart, J. (ed.), Bridges Not Walls (6th Ed.) New York: McGraw-Hill. p. 328

62. I am borrowing the phrases "equipment for living" from Kenneth Burke, whose landmark essay, "Literature as Equipment for Living" is central to my understanding of the communication process.

sending and receiving messages; the process involves engaging in the totality of the relationship of which both verbal and nonverbal messages are a part. It includes not only the subject-at-large, but the entire environment in which the subject exists. This environment is often invisible, but includes the people themselves, the particular purposes of their conversation, the principles underpinning the interaction and the overall performance. Postman uses an organic metaphor to describe this complex process, saying:

> [. . .] communication is not stuff or bits or messages. In a way, it is not even something that people do. Communication is a situation in which people participate, rather like the way a plant participates in what we call its growth. A plant does not exactly grow because it does something. Growth is a consequence of complex transactions among the plant, the soil, the air, the sun, and water. All in the proper proportions, at the proper time, according to the proper rules.[63]

Like marriage, our other relationships are in the midst of a series of changes that produce challenges to intimacy. Screens are not skin. Cell phones cannot effectively channel the nuance of human emotion. These devices have not only altered the way family and friends communicate with one another, but through them, friendships, family relationships and whole communities have changed. Change is inevitable, but no matter the change, there will always be a need for embodied relationships. This might seem to be an odd thing to say. Who can imagine a time when virtual relationships will be preferred over embodied ones? Yet, today, more than ever before, long distance relationships are conducted via the Internet through software platforms and virtual games that allow people to relate to others through avatars, or a second skin. Through masks of altered identities, people spend hours wandering through games such as Second Life, the Sims, and EverQuest, "relating" to other people through their computer-generated self, or their second skin. For the multitudes that enjoy this virtual life, the real world is called "the meat world" and is far too limiting to invest much time. Also, in the past thirty years a new definition of family has come into vogue such that now *family* is often construed as "anyone with whom you are close." Communities were once thought of as the sharing of life together in a given locale,

63. Postman, Neil. (1976). *Crazy talk, stupid talk: How we defeat ourselves by the way we talk and what to do about it.* New York: Delacorte Press.

one where face-to-face relationships could flourish and people could iron out their conflict in the midst of everyday life. This no longer seems to be the working definition of community. Rather, the notion of community has been reduced to a company of people who agree on a particular subject or have a particular hobby in common, such as the faith community, the fishing community, or the gay community. What's more, the experience of friendship is undergoing a change in definition and experience. The design of social networks such as Facebook offer a sort of "friend AutoMat"that is as easy to access as potato chips in a snack machine. Instead of the close circle of affection that is highly dependent upon individuals taking time to be with one another. Now, instead of spending time together, many are satisfied to gather names on a list to add to their roster of friends as in, "I've got 435, how many friends do you have?" Birthdays are announced throughout the network and "friends" chime in from near and far with a quick greeting. Does this reduce the value of a greeting or simply expand the number of ways people are able to say, "happy birthday?" Think about it. What about when a friend posts that they are feeling depressed. A long trail of comments with quick quips such as "hang in there" may be offered, but does this paltry post exempt a friend from actually calling or stepping into the other's life to provide comfort, wisdom, or support? Ultimately, this tendency reduces friends to an image on a wall. Overtime, reducing a friend to an object or a thing instead of persons becomes increasingly pronounced. This trend may be a simple case of the availability of new computer applications and a fast-growing Internet, but it also says something about the ways we are increasingly willing to allow relationships to be reduced to simply shared information. To avoid this ugly trajectory, we must be more intentional about using the communication skills that affirm, encourage, and truly listen to the other. To really communicate *love* we need to remind ourselves that relationships are more than exchanging messages, interacting, or enjoying an animated version of someone. Nor are they the sum of information we collect about another person. Relationships involve actually spending time together. Loving communication with the other begins with receiving the other as other, a true person. Without this, we reduce our friend or lover to a figment of our imagination – something we desire that they be. As Buber explains, "The noblest fiction is a fetish, the most sublime fictitious sentiment is a vice."[64]

---

64. Buber, Martin. (1970). *I and thou.* In Walter Kaufmann (trans.). New York: Scribner. p. 65.

Imaginary People

When we relate to a person as someone who we hope they are, or someone we envision them to be, we are not relating to them as another human being. Instead, we are relating to them as a thing. This is called depersonalization. When we invent a person rather than reckon with who he actually is, we have a difficult time communicating on any deep level because we neglect to listen to what that one is actually saying, and who he actually is. When he says things that are at odds with what we have imagined or hoped he would say, we take offense or feel slighted and are apt to react defensively rather than respond as a mature adult. The problem with loving an imaginary person – someone we have mostly invented – is that it doesn't allow the other to be known. We cannot invent a person in our own likeness and expect the relationship to work. "Loving a fantasy is the greatest barrier to loving a real person." [65] Unfortunately, this is much of the temptation that is occurring with people who have affairs over the Internet. People strike up conversations with someone they've "met" on the Internet and imagine that person is the sum total of how they describe themselves or look in their photographs.

When I consider the complexity of the language of love and the power released in *communicating love* I am encouraged and reminded that no matter how much Western values and cultural mores have changed, the basic fabric of love has *not* changed. No matter the dominant media, government, or the general state of society, when people truly love each other there are natural and normal elements that we can count on. In an ever-changing world we can take comfort in that fact. Above all, love will endure as the motivating force of all life, and relationships are part of the process of communication, a process in which we each have the opportunity to grow. Although one may think primarily of marriage when considering how to more effectively communicate love, friendship is just as important and requires nearly as much focus for the relationship to flourish.

---

65. Smit, Laura A. (2005). *Loves Me, Loves Me Not: The Ethics of Unrequited Love.* Grand Rapids, MI: Baker Academic. P. 172 p. 95.

Intimacy, Mystery, and the Place of Prayer

Intimacy is not only a many-splendored thing, it is multi-layered. There is a "more than-ness" that occurs when people grow close. As an old one-hit-wonder from the 1980s goes, it is "more than just the two of us." We get inklings of eternity in the midst of the closeness. This is not possible unless we remove layers of the outer self. I am not speaking about sexual intimacy here, but – even sexually, intimacy is analogous to true presence. We must remove our clothes. Naked before you I stand. It is the ultimate self-disclosure. We do quite the opposite when we limit our communication with each other to mediated experiences. We add layers through screens, platforms, and symbol systems, which make it all the more difficult to break through to the heart. Masks must be removed for intimacy to grow. Face-to-face communication is the best for this. It takes much bravery to allow the outer layers of ourselves to be peeled away. How does one do this without the strength and grace of God? How does one maintain the patience, endurance, grace, and boldness to begin to know the other, as other?

Earlier I suggested that love cannot be separated from hope and faith in this life, but I have not elaborated on the aspect of faith. When we think of faith in communicating love perhaps the first thing that comes to our minds is faithfulness and trust. These are necessary, but how to we get these? Especially if we have been burned or hurt or grown up in a mistrusting, suspicious, or unloving home? We need prayer.

Prayer and Presence are both essential ingredients to experiencing the other as other. Prayer is not about doing. It is not about obtaining results. It is about communion. Yes, we pray to petition God, to ask him for specific help, but the essence of prayer is not about doing. It is not that we don't want our needs and desires to be met through the Almighty's grace; rather that prayer is so much more than a means to an end. Prayer is not about efficiency. It is about being. Love is much the same way. It is not primarily about doing things for a person or finding someone who can meet our needs. It is not about competing in action to produce results that convince the other that we are "in love." It is about being, being with the other, and being fully present to the other. Prayer and faith are not synonymous; rather, prayer flows forth from faith. As Ellul explains, "Prayer is not a work of faith.

It is a possibility of the work of faith. That is why we are told to pray without ceasing, for faith is completely sterile without this respiration."[66]

Understanding the place of prayer in communicating love to others brings us once again to the place of silence in communication. Silence is the bed of speech. Speech rises out of silence.[67] There, in the reflective, prayerful moments of quietude, we are refreshed and rejuvenated, freed from the bonds of our own limited perceptions and able to move forward in the ever-increasing growth of our relationships toward intimacy. For that, we not only need to think carefully about how we use our communication tools, but we need to take time for solitude so we may bring a more centered, peaceful, and loving self to the other. Here, Henri Nouwen helps us understand that "without the solitude of heart our relationships with others we easily become needy and greedy, sticky and clinging, dependent and sentimental, exploitative and parasitic, because without the solitude of heart we cannot experience the others as different from ourselves but only as people who can be used for the fulfillment of our own, often hidden needs."[68]

So, how can we combat the depersonalization and corresponding lack of authenticity and closeness that our highly technologized society proffers? For one, insistence on physical presence and use of words for everyday talk, rather than opt for ending an easy email or text message. This is part of the way individual volition can still win out over the technological imperative. As you and I take action against the propagandistic technological usurpation of our human faculties we will find hundreds of small decisions every day that make a difference. For example, intentionally waiting until two people can be together in the same room instead of choosing to have an important conversation in public over the cellphone is just one way to make a difference in the social evolution of the technological sway. For some, these small choices may seem laughable. Some may even perceive such action as insignificant – a drop in the bucket, virtually impossible, or technophobia. But, think about how other important

66. Ellul, Jacques. (1973). *Prayer and Modern Man.* Seabury Press. p. 117.

67. Picard, Max. (1952). *The world of silence.* Chicago: Henry Regevery Company.

68. [1] Henri Nouwen, *Reaching Out: The three Movements of the Spiritual Life.* DoubleDay, 1975. p. 30.

matters have been adjusted by individuals changing their attitudes. In the 1970s the campaign against pollution and litter was in full tilt, persuading the public through every available means that littering was hurting our environment. Little by little, the actions of individuals began to affect public spaces and public consciousness began to change. Now it is rare to see someone throwing an empty potato chip bag out of their car window on the highway. It is not only against the law to litter; it has become part of the public consciousness. Jacques Ellul writes that in order to obey the command "watch and pray" . . . "we shall have to conquer ourselves in the face of that gnawing doubt, the continual question, 'what's the use?' It is not merely a matter of wanting to pray, but of praying a genuine prayer. On that score we are caught up in a struggle against the life direction given by our consumer society, which neither knows nor is able to suggest as the meaning of our work, the joy of our life and the value of our society as anything other than a higher level of consumption" (Prayer. P. 144).

In this fast-paced world it is all too easy to brush past the one we love with hardly a word, let alone a hug, kiss, or kind word. In the 1960s the phrase, "take time to stop and smell the roses' was popular. Today, we need to remind ourselves to stop and take time to do the same, especially when in regard to giving and receiving affection.

Chapter 8

The Wellspring

The cycles of Heaven in twenty centuries
Bring us farther from God and nearer to the Dust

If love is ever going to be more than an idea or unrealizable dream it must be worked out in everyday life. It must have hands and feet that put our words and feelings into action. Since the warm and caring feelings that are normally present in love are not always the best indicator of healthy relationship, there must be something more substantial and solid to anchor and uphold the weight of love's glory. It is essential for love to have a way of renewing itself on a regular basis. This is especially so when feelings fade or adversity comes; there must be a means by which we can draw upon love's strength and vigor. Love is more than an idea.

Just as a river flows from a source and does not spring up out of a dead piece of wood or cement sidewalk, so it is with love. Like a river, our human love must flow from a source higher and deeper than itself if it is to water those dry places that are often a part of any long-term love relationship. Think of it: fresh, flowing water does not come out of nowhere. It always has a source. So it is with love. Once discovered, it is essential that love is fed from a generous, unfailing supply. But where is the source or this love? Is there such a supply? The good news is that love is constantly bubbling up out of wellspring of unending supply, and this wellspring of love is the Lord God, Himself. The breadth and length and depth of true love are grounded and rooted in the heart of God Almighty, Creator of the universe – Maker of all. Yes, it is the love of God that provides the fathomless fount for all human loves, and that love is available in infinite, unquenchable supply.

This is because love not only flows forth *from* God; it is part of His nature. The New Testament reminds us that love is not only the Creator's grand idea, but that it is actually the foundation of *who He is.* John, the close companion and disciple of Jesus Christ, explains this when he writes: "Beloved, let us love one another, for love is of God and everyone that loves is born of God and knows God. He that loves not does not know God, for God *is* love. Beloved, let us love one another" (1John 4: 7-8 emphasis mine). That's right –God is the one who thought up love in the first place. As the Author of love, He is also the Source. He *wrote the book of love* and holds the key to every quandary and challenge that love presents.

Even though our human expressions of love are always far less than the perfect love of God, His love remains secure, whole, perfect, unquestionable and without fault. There may not be a direct plumb line to the heart of God in every love relationship undertaken on this great green globe, but there is surely a dotted line, for love cannot exist outside of God. Those who do not know God or acknowledge His Presence in the world are only able to love because He has poured His love out to the world, making it available to us as part of our human makeup. The joy of human love is but a foretaste – or a glimpse – of divine love. It is an inkling of the love of God, and although we humans are prone to corrupt and exploit it, human love always retains something of the nature of God, even if it is the tiniest speck of sweetness and life. Sometimes it takes a major overhaul of the heart for this divine love to begin its work in a relationship, while often it is obscured by layer upon layer of human weakness and frailty. One such frailty is the common experience of fear.

Love and Fear

". . . but perfect love casts out fear." 1 John 4:18

A thick band of fear is often the first layer of frailty to be dealt with by the wellspring of divine love. Of the many reasons that relationships fail, fear is often the one that looms above all others. It distracts us from what really matters, darkens our hearts, and fixes our focus on ourselves. When we open our hearts to love's invitation, it is often fear that closes it. What is it exactly that we fear, and how does it take our hearts captive and steer our attention away from the other? The number of ways could fill an entire book, but here we will contain our discussion to three of the major ones. These include the fear of:

- Rejection

- Loss of self

- Being known

Need I even say a word about the fear of rejection? It is common to all. So common. Rejection comes in all shapes and sizes. It is not simply the wholesale negation or dismissal of relationship that we fear, no. Fear of rejection creeps in quietly like a chilly afternoon mist in late fall. Think of it: If you muster all the courage you can to let your spouse know that you are struggling with jealousy, or that you feel she is spending too much time at work or with her friends, consider how you might feel if she retorts with something ugly such as, "it's because you are so boring," or "my friends are more fun than you are." Rejected, flat out! You'll feel it deeply, and it *doesn't* feel good. We hardly have to wonder why fear can so quickly gain a foothold in our lives. No matter how sturdy the floor of our psyche may seem it is all too easy to feel shaken and unsure when someone we love walks away. This is especially so when we take the kinds of emotional risks that are necessary to stay in open, honest communication.

Early disappointment in life can set the tone for fear of rejection in adulthood. Whether it stems from being the child of a painful divorce or parents who stayed together but couldn't cope with the pressures of raising children, rejection can linger for a lifetime. It taunts us and can keep us from communicating with those we love in life-giving ways. Sometimes fear of rejection is a result of something seemingly insignificant, such as always being last to find a place of acceptance on the playground in grammar school, or picked last for team sports. Rejection does not limit itself to massively painful experiences. It seeps in from the perimeter of our lives and floods our soul, and it hangs around until it is dealt with in a healthy way. The good news is that the predilection in our heart that causes us to live in fear of rejection can be quashed as we come to the deep and living knowledge that we are accepted unconditionally. This transformative knowledge has the power to change our lives, which is why when we experience even a small taste of that acceptance in a relationship with friend or spouse it becomes food for our very souls. Yet, as people come and go in our lives, tramping through the layers of our hearts we are broken over and over again, and the damage these relationships bring often serves to accentuate those deeply rooted feelings of rejection. Instead of growing older and feeling better about ourselves and more capable of maintaining truly loving relationships, the fear of rejection keeps us tied up in childhood knots where we are often our own worst enemies. We do and say things that are often grossly incongruent with our feelings, and sabotage relationships that once seemed so promising. We baffle ourselves and others at our self-defeating behavior. Keeping people at a distance, we wonder why we can't seem to form closely-knit, long-lasting bonds of love. We push the people we love most away and then weep bitter tears for the loss.

The good news is that the chains of fear can be broken, but there is one major dynamic necessary to overcome the fear of rejection, and that is to acknowledge the need for someone with more authority than ourselves to come in and establish the truth of who we are. We need to understand that we are first and foremost people who have been created by a loving Creator, our Father, God. Next, we must come to the realization that we are truly accepted in the Beloved. What does this mean? Those that believe in Jesus Christ, receiving Him by faith as God's answer to the problem of sin, are part of the wondrous and growing people who are known by His Name. It's true! *In Christ*, we are wholly, truly, and unconditionally accepted and loved. Indeed. We have access to the Author of Love through Christ, and do not have to prove ourselves to Him or cajole Him into accepting us. In that knowledge we can stand secure that He will never leave us or forsake us. This knowledge, no matter how much we intellectualize it, must penetrate our hearts. Without this life-giving knowledge we are apt to spend our entire lives driven by the need to avoid rejection. Instead of pressing toward the good, reaching for the prize, going forward – our lives become more informed by a drive to avoid pain, and all our energies are placed into that goal. It's as if pain avoidance becomes our personal mission statement. Unfortunately, the avoidance of pain is not a strong enough motivation to make us good lovers. Living and loving with fear in the lead position will keep us stuck in a rut, or worse, seem as if we are driving a car that can only go in reverse.

A relationship that is steered by fear has little chance of lasting, for instead of optimism, there is exists a quiet belief that in the end, we will be disappointed. It's like living in a house without a strong foundation and a roof that has invisible cracks in it. Undoubtedly, living under this leaky roof of fearful cowering will be anything but comfortable, and it will seriously weaken our ability to communicate love. Instead of kindness, suspicion will reign. Instead of gentleness, accusation will inform our responses. Instead believing the best and cultivating all the underlying attitudes that predispose one person positively toward another, doubt and negativity set the tone for the relationship. Fear of rejection will do this. Unless it is dealt with, fear becomes the very context of the relationship. It becomes the frame that surrounds every encounter, every conversation, and every excursion. It is not a pretty picture.

The fear of loss of self is another deterrent to communicating love and affects each of us in different ways, but for each it involves wrangling with the status of our personal identity. In some ways this fear is a bit like fear of death. No one wants to lose their life. In relationship, when we are pressed to change in ways that seem to compromise who we are we may experience a very legitimate fear of losing our self. On a less dramatic note, this fear may simply be the challenge we feel when a friend or loved one does not appreciate or enjoy the same things we enjoy. Or, the friend we love is always trying to rearrange the things in our lives that we think are important. Think about how you might feel if someone you invite into your home comes in and tries to rearrange all your furniture. Whether its actual tables and chairs or the furnishings of our psychological and emotional makeup, it is one thing to compromise on a particular matter or decision, and yet another thing to allow someone to rearrange your entire life. Fear of loss of self may begin as insidiously as fear of rejection, and does not necessarily begin as a reaction to a domineering partner or parent. This fear is not typically the result of the type of communication behavior going on in a relationship, nor is it one that readily comes to the forefront of most people's minds. It is even more subtle; this fear encroaches, gathering strength in the backwoods our minds, setting the tone for disappointment, suspicion, and control. Fear of loss of self is difficult to identify and not always perceived for what it is, yet this fear is real.

In some relationships, fear of loss of self may show up as a clinging or domineering codependency. People who have been hurt by betrayal, abuse, or domineering relationships often react by keeping their psychological distance in relationships, and fear of losing one's independence – or very sense of self — is often the root. In other relationships it may be mistaken for an unusual need for privacy or independence. There are countless ways that we dig trenches around our heart, creating moats that keep others from getting too close; and we wonder why our relationships always end in some sort of failure or never grow toward true intimacy. These are the chains that keep our hearts in bondage and destroy our ability to stay "in love" for the long term. Unhealthy relationships are often bred from warped self-esteem. Instead of flourishing, the relationship turns inward upon itself and fear takes the driver's seat. Other times, the self-esteem is healthy and in tact, however, love just goes wrong. It is not that love is ever essentially wrong, but it so often corrupted or exploited by human weakness and insecurity that it becomes misery instead of joy. Instead of embracing the other as other, this type of lover may see the friend, spouse, or child as a possession, someone whose sole purpose is to be "there for them." "My friend" becomes *my* friend. "My wife" becomes *my* wife. "My daughter" becomes *my* daughter. This insidious possessiveness that creeps into some of our closest relationships is most common in young children and teens, but it can last a lifetime, nipping at the heels of otherwise mature and well-adjusted adults. Certainly, it is indicative of the cyclical love affairs that plague a person who "really wants to settle down," but hops from one unhealthy relationship to the next. The loss of freedom and self-debasement that often develops in these kinds of perversions of love creates a real fear – one that may easily make a person less likely to open up and avail themselves of love. This leads us to a final fear, and that is the fear of being known.

Some people are closed off from love because they are unfamiliar with the freedom to speak their minds. They don't know how to share who they are with others because they don't really know who they are. They haven't had the opportunity to express themselves, to share who they are in a safe environment. Others have no trouble speaking, but don't know when to be quiet. Both of these behaviors are apt to put up barriers to true love, and neither is healthy. If we ignore the need to self-disclose for the sake of feeling safe and protected we will not be able to do it for long without risking the ruin of relationship. Whether it is a conscious desire or not, the human heart longs to know and be known. This longing is natural; it is a God-given drive. We are social creatures and *we were made for love.* Whether you are an introvert or an extrovert, that longing to be known is an active, motivating force. Yet, the fear of being known – of revealing ourselves to another – is a real one and it can keep us from opening our hearts wide enough to receive *or give love.* In these situations the prospect of being 'found out,' – that is, of another human being discovering all that is on the inside – the good, the bad, and the ugly – is frightening. It is as if there is an inner policeman standing guard at the door of our hearts, and despite a strong desire to relinquish control, we are incapable of opening up to let anyone get beyond the gate. What is the antidote? How are these fears overcome? It always comes back to the wellspring. If we are not in a place of peace with God, knowing we are "*accepted* in the Beloved," it is difficult (nearly impossible) to trust another and allow ourselves to be seen and known for who we truly are. We desperately need the healing properties of God's unquenchable, healing love to wash over us. How easy it is to put a lid on our hearts to protect ourselves from the possibility of disappointment, yet it is that same lid that keeps others from actually getting in. It not only keeps us from communicating love effectively, it truncates our ability to grow toward intimacy. How hopeful it is to know that the fear of being known — the fear of being found out – can be conquered through intimate knowledge of God's love in Christ. Perhaps the most damaging thing is that without understanding *who we are* we have little to bring to others, whether romantically, in friendship, fellowship or serving our neighbor. It is "in Christ" that we slowly discover the truths about ourselves that are necessary to go forward in strength, confidence, *and* humility.

Power and Control

It is impossible to speak about conquering fear without addressing the issue of power and control. Often – *very often* – relationships that fizzle out have their root in the fear of losing control of personal power and autonomy. This, of course, has much to do with the fear of loss of self, but there are times when it is a legitimate concern. When we love someone completely and without reservation we do lose personal power. We see this principle alive in the power of the cross wherein love was exhibited when Jesus willingly offered his own life as a sacrifice to make a way for others to come into fellowship with the Father of Light. There, the overcoming power of love was initiated through death on a cross. Surrendering personal power is never easy, but it is the way toward lasting love. Putting ourselves – that is, our needs, our desires, and our comforts – second, after the other is a good thing, but it is not easy to do. We may never feel terrific about this sort of daily surrender, but, in fact, by surrendering our control we pave the way for rich, satisfying, intimate relationships with those we love.

It may be easy to skip over this section, but I implore you; do not. It is so easy to see the control mechanism operative in others, but just as easy to miss it in ourselves. So I will ask: Do you want to be the one in the driver's seat, making all the decisions, steering the relationship, changing your friend or your partner? If so, it is a good indicator that 'control' is at work in your relationships. If you always have the final say (or want it) you will probably be able to gain that position in the relationship, but that is all you will have. You will not have love. When we love, we give up power. If we have power we give up love. We can have one or the other, but not both. It is either, or. This is because love is about surrender. When we love we place ourselves in the position of weakness, vulnerability. Think of the way Mary of Magdala broke the vile of precious oil over the feet of Jesus. She was giving him more than the traditional foot-washing of biblical times. The oil represented Mary's personal sense of safety and security. In the first century, the oil a person carried with them was analogous to our modern-day life insurance policies. Instead of clinging to this expansive nard, she did not keep anything back, but gave it all to him.

It is not odd that surrender is so unnatural. Surrender is not easy. Yet, when we relinquish the stranglehold of control that so often colors our relationships we open a way for a love that goes well beyond the surface. Consider, again, the cross of Christ – the ultimate surrender – and how it makes a way for people to once again be in fellowship with their Creator. Jesus Himself gave up all his power and esteem to be the perfect sacrifice for sin, even to the point of hanging on a cross and dying a pubic, humiliating death. This utter, total, giving of Himself was a surrender motivated by love.

In our earthly relationships the need for surrender is nearly as important. Although Jesus' surrender of his own life is all-sufficient, in our own relationships we are called to live lives of surrender, preferring one another, in honor. But what does it mean to surrender to another, and is it always appropriate? No, not always. If you are reading this and you are being physically violated or abused, do not surrender to that. Please. Get up. Get help. Get away. But do not leave God out of the mix. He will strengthen and help you. Remember this: The Lord does not call many to martyrdom, and there is only one Jesus. Giving up our control does not usually mean something as dramatic as what Jesus or Mary did, but the power of love in both of these instances is strong enough to subdue us, even when no other human love can. When we surrender to the love of God in Christ we will soon find there is a fathomless well from which we can draw – patience, joy, mercy, kindness, and endurance – enough to last a lifetime. This love spills over into our human loves and has the power to transform them. It cannot remain separate; apart from our human loves. Acknowledging the magnitude of Divine love is a start, but for its power to become manifested in our earthly loves, we must not keep it neatly tucked away – separate from the entirety of our lives. The surrender of which I speak involves the decisions and sacrifices of daily life. Some decisions are surely easier than others such as where to go for dinner or what to make for breakfast, but as the decisions become more difficult, it becomes increasingly difficult to let go of control. If you are married it may involve decisions as life-changing as where you decide to live or what work you choose to do. Whatever your situation, taking a step back to consider the needs and desires of those you love will always involve some kind of sacrifice. Surely, this is opposite from the bulk of messages we receive about love and friendship and it will undoubtedly be a stretch to put this into practice in everyday life, but choosing to trust God with our future frees us from clinging to those we love in destructive ways. When we accept His sacrifice and take Jesus as our own the ache for love that echoes in our souls is finally filled and we can begin to communicate love in ways that are healthy, fulfilling, and life-giving.

Love that Truly Satisfies

When we have tapped into this hidden spring of God's quenchable love we are satisfied. That is because God's love makes us whole. No longer are we compelled to look toward spouse, friend, or mother as the one to meet our need for love. Even though we do need people in our lives, it is tempting to zero in on one of them as our "need-meeter." In Christ, our need for love is met, and as we walk on with Him we will find the unending, splendorous, life-affirming, fecundity of life in relationship with God. As our relationship with God grows our relationships flourish because they are drenched in love – true love – the love of God. No matter how crippling the fear of rejection, fear of losing oneself, or the fear of being known may be, we have the opportunity to choose how we shall live. Each day we awaken with the new chance to overcome the fear, but it must be overcome by drawing from the wellspring of life. Our fears are not easily slain, but the Author of love knows exactly how to slay these dragons in our lives. Each time fear comes in to grip our hearts and we feel the rise of an unloving thought, comment, or behavior coming to the fore, we have the opportunity to come back to the Source of love for renewal and a fresh supply. He is the God of living water. Living water is moving water – water that is stirred. It has a current. It flows daily from the source. This is how we are able to jump into full engagement with people in ways that are life-giving.

Conquering the Fear - Tapping the Source

Surely, if such an unquenchable, fathomless supply of love is available to us, we want to know how to access it, yes? Learning to draw from the source of Love involves knowing God, and this is something that is quite different from simply knowing about Him.

To know Him, we must tap into the wellspring – learn to dwell with Him and give ourselves to Him in ways that are beyond head knowledge. Tapping the source of love means that we will continually be going to God for renewal, refreshment, and allowing Him to fill us with Love. As we "stay current" with God in a relationship that is real, we remain in the refreshment of living water. We are able to wash clean everyday, refresh daily, and become the refreshment to those we love, instead of a drain on them. To dwell in Him we must dwell *on* Him, listen *for* Him, and run *to* Him with all our cares and concerns. He is our Father.

As we know this ultimate, awesome, and amazing Father better, He fills us with love for others and gives us a way to keep a check on the outflow of love to others. Even when our own hearts are like empty buckets, there is an unquenchable supply of love from which to draw. Instead of dry, crusty, weary or empty buckets, our hearts can remain ever full as the love we give to others flows from this limitless, perfect source. How exciting and encouraging this is! To know that a connection with the Author of Love is available and welcome is perhaps the most hopeful of all things, particularly as it pertains to the building and maintaining of our relationships. For it is through the Source of all love that all our loves can be strengthened, renewed, and remain healthy and strong. We are created by God for love's sake and in receiving His love we are able to pour it out more generously to those with whom we have relationship in this world. As we enjoy the benefits of God's love our hearts are filled with love for Him, and we grow in our ability to love others.

Loving God

The idea of loving God may seem a bit foreign to some. Perhaps it is easier to think about believing in God, serving Him, honoring Him, or worshipping Him than it is to think about actually *loving* Him. But loving God involves seeking Him out; it involves taking the time to get to know Him. The fact is, it may be easier to think of God's love for humanity than about our own relationship with Him, but throughout scripture it is clear that God, *our Father*, knows and loves individuals. His love for the world spreads throughout the world, but He looks for – yes longs for – a loving relationship with each of us. As we enter into that relationship we learn that to love Him means much more than to merely believe in Him, obey Him, or serve Him. Loving God involves relating to Him, waiting on Him, — *listening* to Him. It involves communion. The Good News is that, in Christ, we are free to spend time with God. We are free to fellowship with the Author of Love, Himself. As we do, we begin to know the love of God on a level that is much deeper than our intellect. As we seek Him, He fills us with love too deep for words.

Throughout the scriptures our God could easily have depicted Himself as Warrior or Soldier. Instead, the clearest pictures we have of Him are as a Father and a Son. Both are depictions are of a loving family – walking together, working together – with love at the center of all motivation. Even the marriage relationship between one man and one woman is depicted as a "type" of relationship between the Lord and His people. If we endeavor to "go it alone," attempting to let our natural loves carry us through, we end up drawing our strength from a well that runs dry. The resources (emotional, spiritual, physical capacity to "be there") that another person has will never be enough to sustain our need for love, nor will it be enough to sustain our primary relationships. We need to go to the Source and drink deeply from the Well that never runs dry. We all need to let God's love permeate our lives through fellowship with Him. You may be thinking, "my soul is a weary desert. It's no place for God." Let a river run through it, my friend. God specializes in living water. He is the God who provides for His children. He is a God who reveals Himself. Historically, this is so. You may ask, "How do we hear Him?" Is it possible to "hear" God in the midst of this noisy, information-saturated society? Is it possible to make sense of our own thoughts, processing the conversations and knowledge we accumulate throughout each day? He is speaking much more than we might imagine.

Listening Deeply

The same sort of distractions that keep us from listening deeply to others, keep us from hearing God, and while we are called to live in full engagement with each other it is increasingly important to practice a bit of healthy detachment from busyness each day. In fact, if we don't reclaim some quiet space in each day for the precise purpose of listening to Him we may begin to believe that He is silent. Equally disturbing, we will miss the wisdom, love, patience, and direction the Lord is eager to provide as we listen! What a challenge it is to be fully engaged and a friend of solitude, simultaneously. This, too, is a part of the beauty and mystery of all that makes us human. How, you may ask, can we get quiet enough to hear Him? Sitting still, turning the computer and all our other gadgets off, and being fully present to Him is a good place to start. Detaching ourselves from the hectic pace of life is not easy, but even if you are not a busy person, it still may be difficult. It is important to remember that it there is no formula, but there is an invitation. It is recorded that He said it to his disciples in the first century, but the Lord is still saying, "Come to me, all you who labor and are heavy laden, and I will give you rest." Embracing the silence instead of running away from it is a large part of the means by which we can apprehend livingness of our relationship with the Lord, for it is in the quiet of the moment that we are better able to hear the Word of God and lay hold of the refreshing, living waters He has for us. It is here that we are invited to let go of the things that busy us, detach ourselves from the responsibilities of life for a short time each day, and give ourselves to Him in the quiet. David Runcorn's thoughts in this matter bear repeating.

> Detachment is not lack of interest. It is about learning to give space. Mature love is love that has learned to care and offer itself without taking over or possessing. We meet such a love in Christ. In his love we are not dominated. His love delights in drawing out of each of us our own uniqueness but he leaves us free to return his love to the glory of the Father. Detachment enables us to stand back. It enables us to gain a wider perspective. It is not the withdrawal of love and involvement, but a more careful and discerning offering of it. Without detachment a sensitive love for this world, in all its complexity and pain, will be overwhelmed and drained empty.[69]

---

69. Runcorn, David, (1990). *A Center of Quiet.* Intervarsity Press, Illinois.

If we never detach from the cares of this world, they will own us. If we never take a break from the daily responsibilities or wait for a once-in-a-lifetime vacation to slow down, how will we be able to hear Him? How will we know the length and depth, — the breadth and scope — of our Father's love? To sit at His feet and quietly bask in the knowledge of His love is a joy and delight itself, but without spending time there in the quiet, how will our hearts be able to take in the immensity of His great love? Where will we find the strength and patience necessary to truly love others as they are meant to be loved? Soaking in the Presence of the Holy One gives us all that we need to walk in love and communicate it effectively to others, even when we have been offended or treated unjustly.

Forgiveness

The ability to forgive is essential to the maintenance of strong relationships. The bible records for us that Jesus told the questioning follower: Forgive seventy times seven.[70] Whoa! That is a *lot* of forgiveness. Minor offenses may be easier to forgive, but what about the disasters, the disloyalties, the infidelities? These are valid questions, are they not? The words "I'm sorry" or "I forgive you" may be exceedingly difficult to say. It is hard to say "I'm sorry," but even more difficult to offer forgiveness to the one who has deeply offended you. What if the offense is part of a string of offenses that have become a regular feature in our relationship, such as constant lying? Or, the offense may be so egregious that we will take many days or weeks grappling with our feelings, sometimes wrestling them down so that a root of bitterness does not grow up in our hearts. Forgiving someone we love is necessary if we want to continue in any sort of relationship that is life-giving and fruitful, but sometimes the woundedness we feel is so deep it seems we simply cannot possibly forgive, even if we want to. Here we need the help of God and much wisdom.

Offering an apology is one aspect of restoring communion, but how do we learn how to forgive? It may be helpful to remember that whether intentional or inadvertently, everyone is offensive. (Some of us more than others!) The Psalms provide some insight

---

70. Matthew 18: 21 -23.

concerning offense. In Psalms 119, we read: "Great peace have those that love Your law, and nothing causes them to stumble" (Psalms 119:165 KJV). The New International Version, makes it even clearer: "Great peace have those that love thy law and nothing shall offend thee." Nothing? Did the Psalmist say, *nothing*? It is difficult to imagine that we could live in such a state of peace that nothing would offend us, but it seems that it is possible. An alternative way to read that verse is that those who don't allow anything to offend them will have great peace. And, if you think about it, that is even more probable, as well as totally applicable to our ability to walk in love. It is also of immeasurable worth to begin to walk in an attitude of greater humility, remembering that we are not exempt from being offensive, nor are we able to be pleasing at all times to those we love. Perhaps the most significant, yet simple, way to deal with the need for forgiveness is to remain in an attitude of thanksgiving and gratitude toward God for those we love. Again, it is not always easy, but what is there in life that is worthwhile that never presents a challenge?

It is so easy to offend someone, and even easier to remain oblivious that offense has been taken. While we often know immediately if we have hurt someone's feelings or done something that is hurtful or wrong, more often we are unaware. This may be especially so today, as we are each increasingly adapting to mediated communication. When we cannot see someone's body language or hear the tone of their voice we lose those cues that help us interpret what they are feeling. This is why it may be more prudent to keep as much of our conversion in the realm of face-to-face. Could it be as easy as this — simply moving from the digital world of communication to the more visceral one of face to face communication? Probably not. Let's consider, however, just why it may be a major part of the solution. Consider how a child learns a language. Babies do not go to school to learn language at 12 months old. How do they learn? They learn in the context of a family. Watching, observing, modeling, and listening; a child learns to use language through immersion in the life shared with those that love her. And so it is as we learn the language of love.

It is when people are together, sharing life, that the actual meaning of our thoughts and intentions becomes clear. The most effective communication takes place when we are face-to-face, spending time together. As Thomas Kelly wrote, "Knowing a language through ear and tongue is vastly different from recognizing the meaning of written sentences."[71] Our meaning is vivid and life-giving when we share the same space and are immersed in the fullness of each other's presence.

So it is as we endeavor to communicate love. The best place for true dialogue to occur is when we are together. We gain the fullest expression of the other as an authentic other. The gentle nudge, the quiet look, a thoughtful pause or touch – all of these work together much like the ingredients in fresh dough blend and mix as we give it time to rise. And we are right back to the importance of solitude, the intrapersonal and the need for physical presence.

Three Little Words

In thinking about the attitudes and activities that help maintain a peaceful, life-giving relationship there are many aspects of communication that contribute to well being. Specifically, however, I have discovered three that have definitely helped me stay married (and in love) for nearly 30 years. They are just three little words but they make a world of difference, and they are not "I love you." Interestingly, each of these words begins with the letter C, so although I did not set out to create a formula, "the three C's" may be a helpful way to remember their importance in everyday life. Let's look at the way these three words contribute to communicating love.

- ♦ CONSIDERATION

- ♦ CONFESSION

- ♦ COMMUNION

The first sounds so simple that it may seem unnecessary to even mention it, but *consideration* may be the easiest thing to miss. If we can start each day with a willingness and intention to be considerate of the ones with whom we are in relationship, that attitude sets the tone for a loving day. Simple consideration creates mutual positive regard, which is an essential ingredient for a healthy relationship. What does it mean, though, to be considerate? In many ways it means simply to consider the needs of each other as

---

71. Kelly, Thomas. *The Eternal Promise.* USA: Friends United Press. p. ix.

we make decisions and plans, but mostly in the very smallest of ways. Considering the needs and desires of the other goes a long way toward setting the tone for effective, healthy, *loving* communication. When two people are considerate of each other's needs and desires, the room for offense shrinks dramatically. St. Paul emphasizes this dynamic when he explains it to the new Christians gathered in the city of Philippi saying:

> Let nothing be done through selfish ambition or conceit, but in lowliness of mind let each esteem others better than himself. (4) Let each of you look out not only for his own interests, but also for the interests of others. (5) Let this mind be in you which was also in Christ Jesus, who being in the form of God did not consider it robbery to be equal with God, (7) but made Himself of no reputation, taking the form of a bondservant and coming in the likeness of men. (8) And, being found in appearance as a man, He humbled Himself and became obedient to the point of death, even the death of the cross. (Philippians 2: 3-8).

No matter what the relationship, when these values are applied to our day-to-day relationships we not only help transform someone else's gray, wearisome day, but it changes our own outlook. This attitude of the heart and mind helps us to note the little things in our life together such as cleanups, helpful things, going the extra mile, taking an extra few minutes to take care of the other. Thinking of the other first is a great way to practice being considerate of those we love each and every day. This, again, is easier said, than done. Even for people we love most, it is often difficult to defer to the other without taking ourselves into consideration. Surely the context of this passage is of no little import. Paul was writing to those gathered in the Name of Christ Jesus. He was writing to the church, specifically speaking about relationships among Christians.

Whether lack of consideration is at work in the midst of a family, friendship, roommate situation, or marriage, the result is the same: broken communication. Broken communication will eventually mean broken relationship. When we cease to regularly engage in the practice of daily considering the feelings, needs, and concerns of the other, the need for confession comes into the picture. This may be especially true in marriage. Once the initial glow of *Eros* becomes the comfortable, secure, warm relationship of married life it is all too easy to get caught up in the rat-race and forget the "things we knew at first." This is where the practice of daily confession and compassion become critical to "staying in love." The same may be said for *storge* and *philia*. The fires of friendship need stoking from time to time, and families who have fond affection grow cool and distant without the practice of considering each other, in love. We forget; we race through our chores; we try to stuff too many activities into our day, and the ones we love most are often the first to feel neglect. The need for confession becomes especially apparent when we have fallen into this trap.

This is also where the importance of honesty is perhaps most critical. How easy it is to let something small pass, put it away, and forget about it. When we do this we often think that we are rising above the fray – not letting little things bring us down – and surely there are times to take the route of holding one's tongue and letting small things pass, but confession is not only "good for the soul," it is essential if we are to keep the affection and tenderness of a friendship or marriage alive. As we confess our feelings or our sin to one another we make room for communion to be restored. The coming together of one naked personality with another, sharing in the richness of love's delightful treasures is once again restored. Sounds simple, right? Everyone who has lived and loved knows it is not. So what happens when it doesn't work? There is forgiveness again – tiptoeing quietly around the corner – always ready and available to enter the conversation.

The three C's for communicating love don't fall neatly into a rubric or handy guidebook, but they work; they really do. They keep us honest, and honesty is one of the most difficult, while simultaneously important, necessities for communicating love. Living honestly with the ones we love may sometimes be a challenge, but as we are honest with the Lord about ourselves, it becomes easier to live honestly before others. Ultimately, to maintain strong, healthy relationships we must see that all of our human loves must drown in the sea of cultural promise and rise to a higher level. Romantic love, the love of a friends and family, all our loves – must be baptized in the love or God to come to their fullest fruition. Fecundity has as much to do with living a fruitful, flourishing life together as it does with the amount of children who come forth from a man and a woman as an expression of married love. A fruitful life is a happy life. It is a life that gives glory to God and brings meaning and purpose.

Fruitfulness, Freedom, and Meaning

Principles, tips, formulas and methods will not produce a fruitful, flourishing life. How-to manuals will not help either. Our relationships will dissipate like dew on a spring morning if we are not intentional about allowing God's love to be what waters our love. It is not principles that we need. The wise person is, as the German theologian Deitrich Bonhoeffer wrote, the one who is "aware of the limited receptiveness of reality for principles; for he knows that reality is not build upon principles but that it rests upon the living and creating God. He knows, too, therefore, that reality cannot be helped by even the purest of principles or by even the best of wills, but only by the living God."[72] While principles may be used by God as tools, it is the Lord *Himself* we need to invite into our relationships. We must ask him to convert our well-meaning but limited love into one of greater substance – one that is unconditional, one that draws from the source of all love – the Well that does not run dry – that is, God Himself. This love is much more than an idea or a feeling. It is the substance of all things. No matter how much we are tempted to draw from the limitedness of human solutions, the answer to most of our relational issues is spiritual. Thomas Merton's emphasis of this need is put forth in light of the swelling technological wave of the mid-twentieth century, but may be even more salient to our ability to communicate love in our present age. He writes:

> When society is made up of men who know no interior solitude it can no longer be held together by love: and consequently it is held together by a violent and abusive authority. But when men are violently deprived of the solitude and freedom which are their due, the society in which they live becomes putrid; it festers with servility, resentment, and hate. No amount of technological progress will cure the hatred that eats away the vitality of materialistic society like a spiritual cancer. The only cure is, and must always be, spiritual (pp x-xi)[73]

Often, it takes solitude to help us come to grips with the fears that bind our hearts. When we are honest with ourselves about ourselves, honest with God about ourselves, a whole new world of

---

72. Bonhoeffer, Dietrich. (1954). *Life Together: The Classic Exploration of Life in Community*. NY: New York.

73. Thomas Merton, *Love and Need* [in] Merton: Collected Essays (Lousiville: Thomas Merton Center, Bellamine College); September, 1966; Vol. 6, p. 264-266.

possibilities opens up to us and we can move from earthly relationships that are superficial, argumentative, and tenuous, to intimate, long-lasting, fulfilling ones. We need not be afraid of the quiet.

Intimacy

Intimate, long-lasting relationships are built over time, and with great cost. Yet, "it is for this that we came into the world – this communion and self-transcendence. We do not become fully human until we give ourselves to each other in love."[74] Intimacy is built upon much more than our own personal fulfillment and that is the great paradox. Intimacy with others *is* fulfilling, but it cannot be established or maintained if it is cloaked in selfishness. It may take a very long time for our relationships to advance, or it may take a moment, but if we are tending to the soil of our most important relationships and allowing the sun to shine upon them, we stand a much better chance of developing the kind of intimacy and longevity that we desire. For a relationship to grow toward intimacy it must be alive. Growth cannot happen where there is death. Yet, that famous old saying "where there is breath, there is life" holds true. Your friendship or marriage may be hanging onto life by a thread, but where there is breath, there is life, and there is hope for growth.

Whether in the church or at work, in the family or between friends, it is essential to use the means we have of communicating in ways that comport with our desire for communicating love. For instance, the cell phone and other technologies of convenience must be used wisely. Instead of allowing them to use us, we must use them in accordance with our goals. That is, if we value the intensity and close-knittedness of everyday relationships, we must be willing and disciplined to carve out regular face-to-face time for everyday talk. Since we are creatures made in the image and likeness of a marvelous Creator who spoke the world into existence and gave us the ability and privilege of conversing with one another in meaningful ways, it is essential to maintain the integrity of this gift of speech and use it responsibly to manage and maintain the

---

74. Anderson, R., Cissna, K., and Arnett, R. *The reach of dialogue.* (1994). Creskhill, NJ: Hampton Press. p. 250.

relationships that matter most. This necessitates attention to details. What sort of details? Relationship details. While everyone manages their personal relationships uniquely, there are certain aspects of relationship maintenance that are universal, one being that relationship are ongoing; they are always in *process.*

The uncritical acceptance of a 24/7 "always on" mentality fostered by the availability of personal mobile media results in a mental posture devoid of rest, reflection, and quiet repose. In our busy world of rapid information exchange there must be something that silence can add to the nurturing of a well-balanced, productive, and flourishing life. While easy answers are not possible, one may be able to deflate the potential hotbed of problems associated with PMM. The first step must occur on a personal level by refusing to allow the current rhetoric of technology-as-panacea to have bearing in one's life. Awareness that an uncritical acceptance of technology is problematic is a good start. In this, we must remember that it is not the medium itself; it is not the content, nor solely what we do with it which is the most significant factor. Rather, it *is* recognizing how these new technologies intersect with human use to reorganize relationships and, in doing so, redefine for us what things we value, and what things we do not. If this realization does not take place for the individual, the beauty of human speech and relational exchange may land on the endangered species list!

Understanding that God is the source of love and that His love offers us an unending supply of love is perhaps the most fundamental and foundational aspect of all that has been discussed in these short chapters. Whether it is listening with intention, purposing to dialogue in openness instead of argument, or taking time to slow down and talk things over with the people we love — the love of God is available and able to expand the possibilities to all our human loves. Once we are able to apprehend this love of God, we no longer have to go around asking as we did in chapter 1, "Where is the Love?" Going to the root of the Source of Love is the best way to begin to understand how to communicate it with genuine and consistent care. Understanding that a cross is at the center of this magnificent love is essential. True love will never stand the test of time without our making peace with sacrifice, but it is through the Author and Source of Love that we learn the elements of love and begin to get beyond the superficial and into the depths of lasting love in our friendships, families, and married relationships. If we keep looking for love in places other than the Source, the answer may always seem just outside of our grasp, but in truth, it is never more than just a breath away.

Go in peace.

Never forget the cross.

References

Altree, Wayne. (1973). *Why talk? A conversation about language with Walter J. Ong.* San Francisco: Chandler and Sharp Publishers.

Anderson, R., Cissna, K., and Arnett, R. Annett, (1994). *The reach of dialogue.* Creskill, NJ: Hampton Press.

Anton, Corey. *Wide-Eyed* June 2008. Vol. 1 No. 3. CA: Santa Monica.

Birdwhistell, Raymond. (1970). *Kenesics and Context.* Philadelphia , PA: University of Pennsylvania Press.

Bonheoffer, Dietrich. (1954) *Life Together: The Classic Exploration of Faith in Community.* NY: New York.

Bonhoeffer, Dietrich. *Ethics.* (1995). NY: New York. MacMillan Publishing Comp.

Buber, Martin. (1970). *I and thou.* In Walter Kaufmann (trans.). New York: Scribner

Duck, Stephen. (2006). Our friends, ourselves. In Stewart, J. (ed.), *Bridges Not Walls* (6th Ed.) New York: McGraw-Hill.

Durham-Peters, Jon. (1999) *Speaking into the Air.* Chicago, IL: University of Chicago Press.

Eliot, T. S. Choruses from *"The Rock."* *Collected Poems, 1909-1935.* New York: Harcourt, Brace, c. 1936.

Ellul, Jacques. (1973). *Prayer and Modern Man.* Seabury Press.

Ellul, Jacques. (1985). *The Humiliation of the word.* (Trans. Hanks, J.M.) Grand Rapids, MI: Eerdmans.

Floyd, Kory. 2006. *Communicating Affection.* Cambridge University Press.

Gergen, Kenneth. *The Saturated Self: Dilemmas of Identity in Contemporary Life.* USA: Perseus Books, 1991

Haley Burton, Ruth. (2006). *Sacred Rhythms.* Downers Grove, IL: Intervarsity Press

Henri Nouwen Society. *Email list word for the day.* 2009

Henri Nouwen, *Reaching Out: The three Movements of the Spiritual Life.* DoubleDay, 1975.

Kelly, Thomas. (1996) *A Testament of Devotion,* Quaker Publishing.

Kelly, Thomas. *The Eternal Promise.* USA: Friends United Press.

Kelly, Thomas. (1996) *A Testament of Devotion.* San Fransisco: Harper Collins.

Lewis, C.S. (1960). *The Four Loves.* New York: Harcourt Brace & Company.

Merton, Thomas. (1979). "*Love and Need: Is Love a Package or a Message?*" [in] Anderson, R., Cissna, K., & Arnett, R. eds. (1994). *The reach of dialogue: confirmation, voice, and community.* Creskhill, New Jersey: Hampton Pres

Merton, Thomas. (1985) *Love and Living.* Mariner Books

Merton, Thomas. In *The reach of dialogue,* 1994. Anderson, Cissna, and Arnett (1994). Creskill, NJ: Hampton Press.

Merton, Thomas. *Seeds of Contemplation.* p. 41 Thomas Merton, *Love and Need* [in] Merton: Collected Essays (Lousiville: Thomas Merton Center, Bellamine College); September, 1966; Vol. 6.

Meyrowitz, Joshua. (1985). *No sense of place.* New York: Oxford University Press.

Myer, Dick. (2008) *Why We Hate Us.* New York: Crown Publishers

Norris, Kathleen. (2008) *Acedia and Me.* USA: Riverhead Books

Nouwen, Henri J.M. (1990). *Life Signs.* New York: Image Books

Ong, Walter (1981). *The Presence of the Word:* Some prolegomena for cultural and religious history. Minneapolis: Minnesota University Press

Ong, Walter. (1967). *The Presence of the Word.* New Haven: Yale University Press.

Peterson, Eugene. (1997) *Subversive Spirituality,* Errdmans, Grand Rapids.

Picard, Max. (1952). *The world of silence.* Chicago: Henry Regevery Company.

Postman, Neil. (1976). *Crazy talk, stupid talk: How we defeat ourselves by the way we talk and what to do about it.* New York: Delacorte Press.

Rhodes, S.C. (1993). *Listening, A Relational Process.* in Wolvin, A. ed.

Runcorn, David, (1990). *A Center of Quiet.* Intervarsity Press, Illinois.

Shuler, Roger, "Techniques of Touch: New Knowledge about Nurturing Newborns" *UAB Magazine,* Summer 2001 (Volume 21, Number 2). University of Alabama at Birmingham Press.

Smit, Laura A. (2005). *Loves Me, Loves Me Not: The Ethics of Unrequited Love.* Grand Rapids, MI: Baker Academic

Soukup, Paul A., S.J. (2007). *Out of Eden,* Boston: Pauline Books.

Taylor, Charles. (1991). *The Ethics of Authenticity.* Cambridge, MA: Harvard University Press

The Holy Bible, New King James Version. 1992. Thomas Nelson, Inc.

Weil, Simone.(1987) *Gravity and Grace,* NY: Routledge.

Where is the Love?- by Roberta Flack and Donny Hathaway (1971) Lyrics listed at end of the book. Have a listen. http://www.youtube.com/watch?v=6S1-MHhEJxI

Wood, J. and Duck, S. (2006) *Composing Relationships.* CA: Thompson-Wadsworth

Appendix

Interpersonal Online Relationship Development (IORD)

The inception of a model for Interpersonal Online Relationship Development (IORD) first came to me while working on my master's thesis at Monmouth University in W. Long Branch, NJ. It was obvious to me in 1995 that the kind of social interaction taking place online would not be confined to business or government interactions, but had great relevance in the world of relationships. In an attempt to explicate this model I kept coming back to the picture of an ocean wave; this, primarily because the melding of the asynchronous flow of communication in email reminded me of the way a single wave rushes to the shore after it breaks and then rolls back into itself, taking with it whatever debris has been washed onto the shore from an earlier breaker. Of course, waves are not singular. They are not separate events rising up outside of the wider body of water. While they rise and fall and appear to be single waves, they are connected to the full scope of the sea, mingling with water molecules in the depths and across the far reaches of the entire ocean. So it is with wireless communication. Emails may be addressed to individuals but they travel long and far across continents, forwarded to miscellaneous unknown parties, and remain in record, forever.

The IORD model seemed to be helpful to me as well because online relationship development is somewhat akin to the undulating motion of a living body of water, with waves rising up out of the deep (the disclosure of the true self) and breaking in upon the shore (the screen, or inbox), gathering up what was left from a prior wave crashing (shells, dead fish, sea glass, garbage and sundry debris). Any "individual" way is obviously so much a part of the collective body that the debris could have initiated from just about anywhere in the world. So it is with email communication, text-messaging, social networking, viral videoing, etc.

Initially, I did not advance this model because it seemed so simple, but it appears that my thoughts on the matter were somewhat discerning, for with each advance in technology, the devices being used for interpersonal communication have proliferated, presenting the opportunity for relationships to develop online overtime, accumulating in depth and breadth just as a wave does when the tide changes. And, as self-disclosure advances across multiple channels, using an increasingly wide variety of communication cues from voice (cell phone and skype) to sight (profile photos, instant messaging) discussions undulate and morph, sometimes into confrontations and flame wars; other times into genuine friendship, even marriage.

The conversations in this digital environment are liquid, just like water. They rarely move in linear fashion, but crash in upon each interlocutor with ripples, great and small, much like the breakers crashing upon the shore. No matter where they seem to start, the interactions always turn back in upon themselves, often getting lost in the deep of the human mind and daily work cycle, mingling with everyday activities, dissolving in the huge pool of unexplored psyche of individual interlocutors. Because conversations ebb and flow through self-disclosure and overtime advance to relationship, the true depth cannot be precisely studied because this ebb and flow is part of the mystery of relationship. While conversation analysis and research on perceived depth of relationship all have their part in uncovering the level of relationship richness, the most these studies can do is point to patterns. Relationships cannot (must not) be relegated to a slab of marble in a lab room. They are part of the holy circle of life, the best part of the human experience – one that cannot be confused with formulas and percentage points.

Finally, the myriad nonverbal communication cues that are missing in mediated settings contribute greatly to the advancement of relationship, and cap off my understanding of the wavelike motion in IORD. Because the nonverbal cues are largely unavailable online, what manifests between two people has more of an appearance of relationship than an actual relationship. A posted image helps broaden the view of the other as much as using skype, but no application provides the needed full scope of communication. Ultimately, then, in online discussions, the process of relationship development is transferred to a setting that is artificial, yet it can still flow. A semblance of relationship may appear, but knowledge of the other consists more in an ambient awareness than actual relationship. Because the words are symbols they can transfer to alternative settings, and depending upon how much any one person brings into the discussion, there will be a similar undulation and flow. Over time, particularly as online conversations expand to other channels, such as voice and face-to-face visits, the relationship has the potential to gain more strength and authenticity. Simple, but I've never noted it until now.

"Lord in my zeal for the love of truth, let me not forget the truth about love. "

Thomas Aquinas

"Lord in my zeal for the love of truth, let me not forget the truth about love. "
Thomas Aquinas

"Lord in my zeal for the love of truth, let me not forget the truth about love. "

Thomas Aquinas

"Lord in my zeal for the love of truth, let me not forget the truth about love. "
                                    Thomas Aquinas

"Lord in my zeal for the love of truth, let me not forget the truth about love. "
Thomas Aquinas

"Lord in my zeal for the love of truth, let me not forget the truth about love. "
                                                                Thomas Aquinas

"Lord in my zeal for the love of truth, let me not forget the truth about love. "
Thomas Aquinas